Geirangerfjorden →
Strynevatnet
Lake
← Eilean
Donan Castle
• Brugge
Neuschwanstein Castle
LOIRE
VALLEY — □ • Paris •
EUROPE   • The Tirol
         • Venice

Thira

• Tafraout

Pyramids
of Gîza

AFRICA

ASIA

Beijing •

Hunza Valley

Mount
Fuji
Kyoto • +

Dal Lake → ← Mount
           Everest
                   • Lhasa
Huang Shan
Mtns.

□ BHUTAN

Taj Mahal •

PACIFIC

OCEAN

• Bangkok

→ EAST
  AFRICA

Etosha
Nat. Park
    • Victoria
      Falls

Namib Desert

INDIAN

OCEAN

YOUNG TOURIST DONS MANDARIN ATTIRE AT BEIJING'S FORBIDDEN CITY.

EXCURSION TO
ENCHANTMENT

A Journey to the World's Most Beautiful Places

Prepared by the Special Publications Division
National Geographic Society, Washington, D.C.

EXCURSION TO ENCHANTMENT
A Journey to the World's Most Beautiful Places

Contributing Authors: CHRIS ECKSTROM LEE,
PAUL MARTIN, TOM MELHAM, THOMAS O'NEILL,
CYNTHIA RUSS RAMSAY, JENNIFER C. URQUHART
Contributing Photographers: TOM BEAN,
ANNIE GRIFFITHS BELT, PAUL CHESLEY,
NICHOLAS DEVORE III, MEDFORD TAYLOR
Map Artist: SUSAN M. JOHNSTON

Published by: THE NATIONAL GEOGRAPHIC SOCIETY
GILBERT M. GROSVENOR,
President and Chairman of the Board
MELVIN M. PAYNE, THOMAS W. MCKNEW,
Chairmen Emeritus
OWEN R. ANDERSON, *Executive Vice President*
ROBERT L. BREEDEN, *Senior Vice President,*
Publications and Educational Media

Prepared by THE SPECIAL PUBLICATIONS DIVISION
DONALD J. CRUMP, *Director*
PHILIP B. SILCOTT, *Associate Director*
BONNIE S. LAWRENCE, *Assistant Director*

Staff for this book
PAUL MARTIN, *Managing Editor*
CHARLES M. KOGOD, *Illustrations Editor*
CINDA ROSE, *Art Director*
MONIQUE F. EINHORN, REBECCA LESCAZE,
Researchers
VICTORIA COOPER, LINDA HILL, *Research Assistants*
RICHARD M. CRUM, CHRIS ECKSTROM LEE,
PAUL MARTIN, TOM MELHAM,
THOMAS O'NEILL, CYNTHIA RUSS RAMSAY,
JENNIFER C. URQUHART, *Picture Legend Writers*
JOHN D. GARST, JR., D. MARK CARLSON,
SUSAN I. FRIEDMAN, *Map Production and Research*
H. ROBERT MORRISON, *Editorial Consultant*
ROSAMUND GARNER, *Editorial Assistant*
SHARON KOCSIS BERRY, *Illustrations Assistant*

Engraving, Printing, and Production Manufacture
GEORGE V. WHITE, *Director,*
Manufacturing and Quality Management
VINCENT P. RYAN, *Manager, Manufacturing*
and Quality Management
DAVID V. SHOWERS, *Production Manager*
KEVIN P. HEUBUSCH, *Production Project Manager*
LEWIS R. BASSFORD, *Assistant Production Manager*
KATHY CIRUCCI, TIMOTHY H. EWING,
Senior Production Assistants
CAROL R. CURTIS, *Senior Production Staff Assistant*
SUSAN A. BENDER, BETSY ELLISON,
MARISA FARABELLI, KAYLENE KAHLER,
KAREN KATZ, SANDRA F. LOTTERMAN,
ELIZA MORTON, DRU STANCAMPIANO,
Staff Assistants
BRYAN K. KNEDLER, *Indexer*

*Sleepy lions take the sun in Kenya's Amboseli National
Park.* PRECEDING PAGES: *Mount Fuji, Japan's highest and
holiest mountain, keeps lordly sentinel over the island of
Honshu. The Japanese view the 12,388-foot volcano as the
meeting place of heaven and earth.* HARDCOVER: *Exquisite
lines identify the Taj Mahal.*

HARDCOVER ILLUSTRATION: MARK SEIDLER; PAGE 1: DAVE BARTRUFF;
PRECEDING PAGES: NATIONAL GEOGRAPHIC PHOTOGRAPHER GEORGE F. MOBLEY

CONTENTS

M uted colors proclaim the Scottish Highlands, where a sea loch surrounds Eilean Donan Castle, near Dornie opposite the Isle of Skye. Built around 1220 to ward off Danish raiders, the castle today welcomes visitors from April to September.

HIBISCUS BLOSSOM FLOATS ON PELLUCID WATERS OFF ELEUTHERA ISLAND IN THE BAHAMAS.

AN INTRODUCTION

By Paul Martin

A gentle breeze rolls in from the sea, rustling the stiff fronds of coconut palms edging the beach. Sitting in the shade of a palm tree, I look out on a seascape of luminous colors. At anchor on the tiny bay before me are a dozen gleaming sailboats, their hulls slashes of white on a backdrop of startling blue. A curving brushstroke of golden sand defines the semicircular bay. Set back from the beach, dense tropical growth spatters the surrounding hills in the sensuous greens of an impressionist's palette. I am in a traveler's paradise such as dreams are made of. This sunny speck of tranquillity is the island of Mayreau, part of the Grenadines, a 50-mile chain of unspoiled isles divided between the countries of St. Vincent and Grenada. Tucked away at the southern end of the West Indies, the Grenadines separate the Caribbean Sea from the Atlantic Ocean. The island nation of Barbados lies to the east; the next stop beyond — Africa.

I have come to Mayreau on an excursion to enchantment, a journey to one of the world's beautiful places. Earth abounds in such settings — from lush river valleys to grassy plains, from lofty mountains to wild coastal realms. But spots such as Mayreau are special. For me, as for many others, islands represent a place to kick off your shoes and indulge in Robinson Crusoe fantasies. On Mayreau, those fantasies can come true, if only temporarily. For a week, I settled into that special way of living perfected by islanders — where the quickest pace of the day is a sunset stroll along the beach. I soon found that decisions on this 700-acre hideaway are few and elemental: Should I take a swim just now? Get back into that suntan-oil-smudged paperback? Or maybe just sit here under this palm tree for a while longer.

"What most people do here is *nothing* — absolutely nothing," said Undine Potter with a laugh. Undine, along with her husband, Tom, runs the Saltwhistle Bay Resort, the only hotel on Mayreau. "People come here just to get away, to relax." And get away they do. On Mayreau there are no cars, roads, or telephones. The only way to get here is by boat — or by swimming. (Undine shook her head over the story of one sunstruck fellow who did attempt to swim from Mayreau to a neighboring island. They searched for him for hours before hauling him out of the ocean, somewhere en route to Africa.)

Tanned and relaxed herself, Undine told me that she and Tom bought the 22 acres for their resort in 1977. She's originally from Germany, Tom from Canada. "We lived here in a tent at first, until we got our house built." Today, a cluster of stone bungalows — 20 guest rooms in all — stands amid a garden of red poinsettias, oleanders with bright pink blossoms, and an assortment of fruiting trees: papaya, soursop, tamarind . . . lemon, lime, orange. All about the grounds, sea grape and palm trees cast islands of shade on a wind-rippled sand sea. The sounds are those of nature — the rush of wind through the trees; the songs of small, brightly colored

Magical light bathes the southern Aegean, where a church clings to a cliff on Thíra, a volcanic Greek isle also known as Santorini. Worlds unto themselves, islands everywhere beckon travelers with the promise of an escape to the unusual.

birds; the gentle wash of surf. Near the beach is an open-air restaurant and bar. Each night, as calypso music played and a breeze blew in off the Atlantic, I dined there on seafood pulled hours earlier from the surrounding waters, a bounty of grouper, red snapper, lobster, or conch.

Like most guests at Saltwhistle Bay, I spent my days near the beach. But I also enjoyed Mayreau's other sights. A steep half-hour hike from the bay leads up to the island's village, where 170 or so people live, mostly fishermen and their families. Perched on the highest point on the island, the village gives a windy, sweeping view of the entire Grenadine chain. Between St. Vincent to the north and Grenada to the south, the tiny islands of the Grenadines lie scattered like a handful of emeralds cast upon a shimmering blue tabletop.

I sailed one day to a nearby cluster of islands, the Tobago Cays. After we anchored in swimming-pool-clear shallows protected by a surrounding reef, I donned snorkeling gear and slipped into a natural aquarium. Paddling slowly about I could see fish of seemingly limitless variety. Gaudy colors competed with bizarre shapes for my attention. Squadrons of small, nearly transparent fish worked diligently on their maneuvers, alternately practicing right faces and left faces just inches from my hand.

The Grenadines, blessed with a wealth of safe anchorages and near-constant breezes, offer one of the world's best sailing grounds. At any time, I could count several boats on the horizon, from small sloops to ships out of another age. One sight I'll always remember is that of a graceful four-master ghosting along under full sail as the setting sun tinted the sky in lavender and orange.

In contrast to the slow pace of life on Mayreau, my stay there sped quickly to an end. As I left this haven, I thought of other islands I have visited: the Florida Keys, the Bahamas, the Virgin Islands, the Hawaiian Islands. I recalled munching on bollos—spicy Cuban fritters—while ambling down the narrow streets of Key West, one of Ernest Hemingway's favorite haunts. In the Bahamas, I found a coral wonderland while diving in the Tongue of the Ocean off Andros Island. And a week's sailboat cruise among the U.S. Virgins convinced me that the territory deserves the slogan appearing on its auto tags: "American Paradise."

When it comes to an island paradise, however, few surpass the Hawaiian chain. There you can marvel at the earth itself being renewed, as I did when I watched orange-hot lava from Hawaii's Kilauea volcano spread down a slope during an eruption. You can witness the majesty of a humpback whale breaching in the waters off Maui . . . or savor the lushness of a rain forest dripping with moisture and ablaze with fiery red blossoms of the 'ōhi'a tree. After seeing such wonders, you'll understand why Hawaiians assure departing visitors that they will return.

Islands the world over exert that sort of pull. My own travels have touched on just a few of earth's island treasures. A dream itinerary would also have to include the storied Greek isles, the islands of the South Pacific, and many other places where blue skies, warm breezes, and gentle surf beckon.

As alluring as such getaways may be, they are only part of the excursions offered in this book. In the five chapters that follow, our writers and photographers travel the continents—to Europe, Asia, Africa, South America, and North America. Their essays and photographs present a varied sampling of the world's most scenic locales. Not all their destinations proved as restful as my island idyll. Some were physically demanding. But, whether trekking through a remote region of Bhutan or bouncing along a rugged mountain track high in the Andes, our writers and photographers all were moved by the uncommon beauty of the places they visited.

Each chapter opens with an in-depth look at one particular area of the continent being featured. In Europe, writer Jennifer Urquhart and photographer Annie Griffiths Belt travel through France's picturesque and historic Loire Valley. They explore a domain of châteaus and abbeys, walled towns and vineyards—a place where "luminous light . . . bathes gentle, green terrain." Over the centuries, this landscape "has enchanted kings and poets," including François I, who built the 440-room château of Chambord, "the grandest of all the pleasure palaces of the Loire." The Loire also reveals its charm in less flamboyant ways: On a cycling trip outside Tours, Jenny Urquhart passed "Peonies and poppies in full bloom snuggled against farmhouses that looked old enough and mossy enough to have grown right out of the earth."

Shifting to Asia, we focus first on Bhutan, a kingdom "sequestered in the eastern reaches of the mighty Himalayas." Writer Cynthia Ramsay and photographer Paul Chesley journey to this land where time seems to have stood still. "Until just a few years ago," observes the author, Bhutan was ". . . a medieval society in which monks had a monopoly on learning, serfs raised what was needed on feudal estates, and everyone worried a lot about demons and evil spirits." Even though Bhutan has begun to open its doors to the outside world, it remains "somehow special, beckoning the traveler with the enchantment of the remote, the barely attainable."

Highlighted in Africa is the Great Rift Valley region in Kenya and Tanzania. Writer Chris Eckstrom Lee and photographer Medford Taylor roam "a land of lemon-gold grasslands . . . huge soda lakes . . . lone mountains wrapped in snowy capes that rise above equatorial forests, and apocalyptic desert moonscapes." On their safari, they range across the Serengeti, where Masai tribesmen follow their traditional ways. There, Chris Lee witnesses a "treasury of African wildlife: Cape buffalo grazing along a river; giraffes poking up through tall acacias; lions lounging on the plain." From the teeming game sanctuary of Ngorongoro Crater to snow-capped Mount Kilimanjaro, East Africa reveals "a showcase of . . . natural wonders."

In South America, writer Tom Melham and photographer Nicholas DeVore III explore the lake region of Chile and Argentina, a realm that "offers an impressive, often contradictory, variety of forms: volcanoes and glaciers, dense forests and open rangelands, rocky seacoasts and hills patchworked into farms and woodlots." In the resort of Bariloche, we see chalets built by Swiss and German immigrants. On isolated Chiloé Island we pause where naturalist Charles Darwin stood in 1835 as he witnessed "the 'magnificent spectacle' of Osorno, a mainland volcano some 80 miles away, in full eruption." We also visit the Patagonian cattle country that once was home to a pair of displaced Yankees—Butch Cassidy and the Sundance Kid.

Finally, in North America, we visit the famed Inside Passage of British Columbia and Alaska—"a thousand miles of wild coast." Along with photographer Tom Bean, writer Thomas O'Neill travels the Marine Highway between Seattle and Skagway. "What is most striking of all . . . ," he writes, "is the immediacy of the wilderness: mountains rearing out of the sea; trees, thick as feathers, growing right to the waterline." Ashore, we prowl the misty forests of British Columbia's Queen Charlotte Islands, home to the Haida Indians. On Admiralty Island we watch Alaskan brown bears feasting on salmon. Then we head north to the "stark, dominating wilderness" of Glacier Bay, where "ice grinds and carves."

In addition to the areas presented in depth in this volume, the five chapters include portfolios of photographs from other locations. In image after image, the beauty of earth's special places shines forth. Together, the text and photographs that follow offer a true excursion to enchantment. 🏔

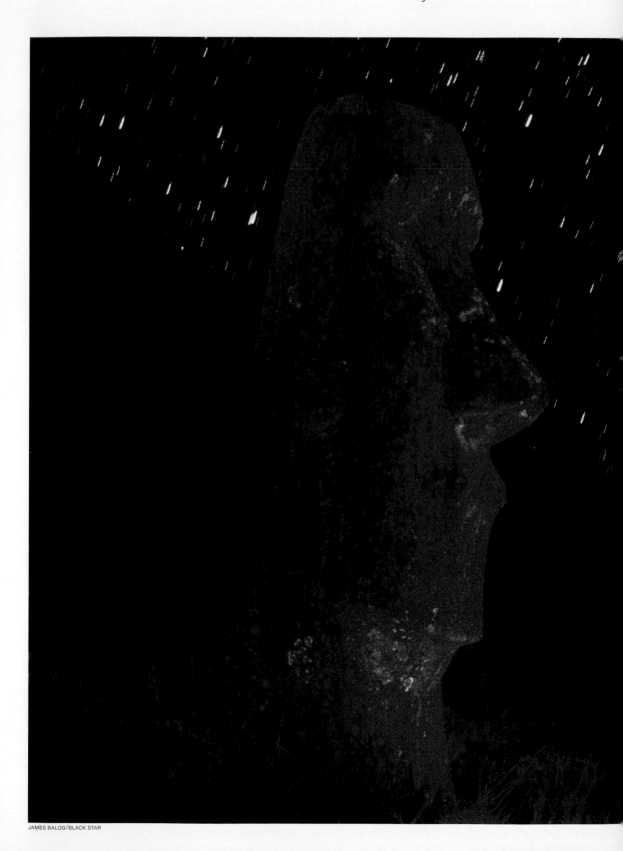

ilent sentinels guard the mysteries of Easter Island. Overhead, Halley's Comet marks time's slow passage on this lonely isle in eastern Polynesia. More than 800 giant stone statues have reposed here for centuries, testimony to the glory of the island's ancient chiefs.

HALEAKALA CRATER
Hawaii

Witnessing a world of wonder daily born anew, a visitor on Maui (above) gazes at sunrise over the 10,023-foot-high crater of Haleakala, House of the Sun in Hawaiian. The volcano, with its 19-square-mile crater, stands as the massive centerpiece of Haleakala National Park. Haleakala last erupted in 1790. In this fantasy landscape rare silversword plants (right) thrive in the rocky soil below cinder cones left by secondary eruptions. Relatives of the sunflower family, silverswords grow only on the islands of Maui and Hawaii. In its lifetime of up to 20 years, the silversword produces a single tall stalk topped by purple blossoms; soon after, the plant dies.

AITUTAKI
Cook Islands

Tranquillity of the South Pacific enwraps strollers on tiny Aitutaki, one of the Cook
Islands. Named for the British explorer James Cook, who visited them in the 1770's, the
15 volcanic isles and coral atolls spread across 750,000 square miles of ocean.

COTTON COULSON

Caribbean jewels, the Grenadines offer the enchantment of blue waters, murmuring surf, and golden sands. Off the Tobago Cays, foreground, a surrounding reef shelters crystalline shallows. In the distance lie Mayreau, right, and Union Island, left.

SHINING JEWELS

SUPREME CHÂTEAU OF FRANCE'S LOIRE VALLEY, CHAMBORD GLOWS AFTER A SPRING STORM.

LOIRE VALLEY

By Jennifer C. Urquhart
Photographs by Annie Griffiths Belt

"Soft" is a word heard often in the Loire Valley. Sometimes it speaks of the pleasing quality of life and the agreeable nature of those who live in France's heartland. Or it might describe the *tendre tuffeau,* the soft, chalky white stone quarried here for centuries to build the châteaus and walled towns for which the region is famous. But more often "soft" speaks of an appealing landscape: of the luminous light that bathes gentle, green terrain, where river, trees, sky, all blend in the moisture-laden air. It is hard to tell where river leaves off and trees and meadows begin, or to find the edge of trees against the sky.

It is a landscape that beguiles over time, rather than captivating at first glance. Through the centuries it has enchanted kings and poets, and it still charms those fortunate enough to travel here. For me the enchantment of the Loire Valley would come in its castles, of course, and in its rolling pastoral beauty. But it would be as much in a medley of small delights that please all the senses: the taste, the first morning after I arrived, of rich and fruity apricot jam on a flaky croissant, bringing back in a flash my first travels in France, many years before as a student. It would be in the heady scent of wisteria and lilacs in full bloom, in gardens, over walls, everywhere. And of roses—golden-pink and crimson climbing trellises in every village and town. It would be the cheery *"bonjour madame,"* and beaming smile of a farmer in his asparagus field. Or schoolgirls bidding farewell with the traditional kiss on each cheek. And a silver-haired man on a bicycle riding carefully home one-handed, with the other arm securely around three fresh *baguettes*—the long loaves essential to any French meal. Or the dignified brown poodle that greets guests at one restaurant with the air of a gracious host.

Upstream at its beginnings, the Loire River is anything but soft, pouring off a volcanic mound high in the Massif Central and cascading through rugged mountainous terrain. France's longest river, the Loire flows northward for more than half its 600 miles. By the time it turns for its westward run to the Atlantic, through what is generally known as the Val de Loire—from just above Orléans to beyond Angers— the river has settled into a more leisurely pace, and begun to pick up such appealing tributaries as the Cher, the Vienne, and the Indre.

I had headed south from Paris in late afternoon, across the flat expanse of the Beauce, France's grain belt. Fast-moving clouds played light and shadow across fields of brilliant yellow rape flowers and pale green young wheat. Farmhouses rose, high and square at the edge of fields. Church steeples, matched by poplars in martial rows, marked distant villages. Now signs indicated a château, a vineyard, an abbey—or the possibility of a leaping deer. I was nearing the Loire Valley, where France's kings and nobles came to hunt and enjoy life and to build their castles secure from the wars and political tumult that plagued Paris and the rest of France. Even so,

Open window invites a neighborly exchange in the village of Savonnières. Five-year-old Lucie de Lestang brings roses to the Caillaud sisters and cuddles Fifi, their pet guinea pig. Such intimate encounters come often in the Loire, a pastoral realm that has long captivated visitors.

here took place some of the greatest acts in France's history: turbulent upheavals that finally brought unity and a national identity. Actors on this grand stage include those whom France and England shared—the Plantagenets: Henry II and Richard Cœur de Lion, Eleanor of Aquitaine—and some who belonged only to France, soldier-saint Jeanne d'Arc, Louis XII, and François I.

Near Orléans I caught my first glimpse of the river, broad and shallow, weaving its way through sinuous golden-pink sandbars, lapping at willow-edged banks. "Murmuring in low tones," in the words of one poet, at times it "Flings its curving arms around a beguiling isle." The Loire is not always so indolent. With heavy rains it can swell to a torrent. Much of the road I would follow runs on both sides of the river atop high levees, built to keep back floods that once rampaged.

I first encountered Jeanne d'Arc in Orléans. On a white horse, she headed a parade much as the real Jeanne must have led her faithful comrades into Orléans on May 8, 1429, after she raised the siege of the town, thereby turning the tide of English domination in France. But that's getting ahead of her story, for she had been all over the Loire region: to the church of Sainte-Catherine-de-Fierbois, where she found her sword; to Chinon, where she found her *gentil Dauphin*—the heir to the throne; to Loches, where she implored him to go to Reims to be crowned Charles VII. "There is no place in the region she didn't go," said one man I met in Orléans, which was gearing up for the annual commemoration of the Maid's arrival.

As darkness fell, candles in niches of the facade of the cathedral of Sainte-Croix flickered all the more brightly. A ceremony that has gone on each year for more than five centuries began. The mayor presented the banner of Jeanne d'Arc to the bishop, who carried it into the cathedral. "A beautiful star in our history," the bishop called Jeanne. Choirs sang; trumpets sounded; bells tolled. It was after midnight when the crowd dispersed quietly into the night. I found a nice irony in the cathedral the next morning. A small chapel honoring Jeanne is right next to a memorial to the British soldiers who died in France in the First World War.

Seventy miles downstream from Orléans in the city of Tours, almost at the center of the Loire Valley, I met Jacques Davidson and his wife, Zabeth, who have resided for decades in the region. On a bright spring Sunday, we strolled from their 16th-century house in the heart of the medieval town. Fluffy white seeds wafted on a breeze like so many tiny parachutists. Zabeth, an energetic woman in her 70s, darted ahead in the narrow streets to show her favorite aspect of some of the ancient houses, the ornately carved stairways that climb the outside walls.

The Davidsons take great pleasure in showing off their region. Together, we drove along the valley of the Manse River, a tributary of the Vienne. This green rolling countryside would become my favorite area of the whole Loire region. The horse chestnuts were in full bloom. At times a château or a manor house would peek from a grove of trees or a village would loom on a ridge. Zabeth pointed out a *pigeonnier*. Before the French Revolution, these squat dovecotes housed pigeons reserved for the tables of the nobility. The number of pigeons an individual seigneur, or noble, could keep was limited by the size of his landholding, perhaps one pair per half acre. In a kind of disguised—and greatly hated—tax, the pigeons fed off the fields of peasants, who were not permitted to touch the birds. We wound through vineyards. Magpies flashed black and white in hedges. We skirted Chinon itself, where the towering, ruined château-fortress high on a ridge dominates the town below, then turned toward Candes-Saint-Martin.

Swelled by tributaries such as the Vienne, the Indre, the Cher, and the Loir, the Loire River sweeps toward the Atlantic through the broad valley region known as the Val de Loire. Along the way, the river skirts vineyards, abbeys, châteaus, and ancient walled towns.

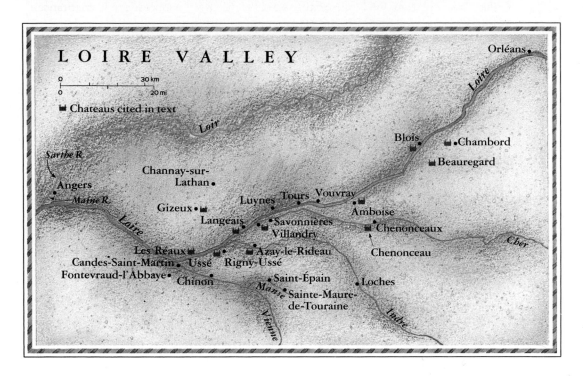

It seems that Jeanne d'Arc is not the only soldier-saint in this region. A thousand years before Jeanne, in the fourth century, a Roman soldier named Martin—known for cutting his coat in half to share it with a shivering beggar—was converted to Christianity, eventually serving as bishop at Tours. It was, however, downriver at Candes that the bishop died in A.D. 397. Thinking themselves fortunate to have the remains of such an illustrious personage, the local people determined to keep the remains at Candes. But the good Christian citizens of Tours came in the dead of night, and, through a church window, snatched the body of their beloved St. Martin. Legend has it that as Martin's body proceeded upriver by boat, trees bloomed, even though it was November. And in France now, what we know as Indian summer is called the Summer of St. Martin.

In Candes, we climbed a steep, cobbled street past the church and soon were relaxing in wicker chairs on the terrace of an 18th-century bishops' residence. The house now belongs to Leva and Janine Katchatouroff, who live in Paris. But weekends they spend here. "Some say it is sleepy country here," said Mme Katchatouroff. "Soft . . . it's a soft region." I sipped the deliciously smooth peach wine that she makes. In fir trees nearby *tourterelles,* turtledoves, cooed gently. "I love it when they come back each spring," she said. The sun gradually set, turning fleecy white clouds to pink and gold, and the drifting waters of the Vienne and the Loire to silver as they merged below us.

The great French novelist Honoré de Balzac loved the Loire Valley and did much of his writing here. He wrote of the region's special enchantment—in particular of the turreted châteaus of Touraine, which he described as "ivy clad, standing among . . . groves of mulberry trees and vineyards . . . mirrored in the Loire."

One might well ask, what exactly is a château? And why are there so many

27

in the Loire especially? It's true that in the Renaissance they became pleasure palaces for a privileged nobility. But the English word "castle" and the French word "château" both derive from the Latin *castellum,* a diminutive for *castrum* or fortified place. The early châteaus were indeed fortresses, often built upon earlier Roman strongholds. Towers and crenellated walls set on high bluffs presented a formidable visage in a time of fierce power struggles among petty seigneurs.

"That's why France has so many châteaus," commented an Englishwoman, the wife of a retired army officer. She spoke a touch smugly—Anglo-French rivalry is not dead. "We in England have been unified for so much longer. They had all that fighting here."

With the strengthening of the French monarchy by the end of the 16th century, however, such turmoil abated. And what had been a fortress-castle was modified into an open dwelling. Moats once used for defense became reflecting pools to enhance the castle. As the need to defend territory diminished, members of the French aristocracy vied with each other in the Loire to build ever more splendid domiciles. It is these, bearing lilting names like Beauregard, Chenonceau, Azay-le-Rideau, that are the stuff of dreams. And, of course, there is Chambord.

Rain in sheets moved rapidly down one *allée* through the forest. Gusts of wind swirled leaves in a darkening sky as the storm approached. I watched from the roof of Chambord, the hunting lodge to end all hunting lodges, the grandest of all the pleasure palaces of the Loire, and the ultimate symbol of the power of François I. The château has 440 rooms and absorbed with ease the 2,000 people who swarmed below for a champagne reception. But for me the roof was a delight. With its 365 chimneys and 800 capitals, myriad gables and cupolas—inlaid or adorned with cherubs and posies—the roof has been likened to the skyline of Constantinople. A fellow guest standing near me had another idea. "It is a *gâteau,* a huge cake."

From the roof, the women of the court would watch the hunters returning and socialize among themselves. For François I liked to have women around. "A court without women is like a year without spring," he would say, "and a spring without roses." Begun around 1519, Chambord took more than 15 years to build. It must have impressed the Holy Roman Emperor Charles V, who visited in 1539, for he called the château the "epitome of human industry." Or it might have been the welcome François I laid on that pleased the emperor—"a swarm of young women dressed as Greek goddesses who ran in front of his horse and strewed his path with flowers." But now the rain reached us on the roof and drove us down Chambord's famous spiral staircase, lit by hundreds of little candles in glass cups.

What Chambord offers in size and boldness, such châteaus as Azay-le-Rideau and Chenonceau equal in grace and delicacy. Indeed, Chenonceau is called the "Ladies Castle," for the women who helped create it. Late afternoon was my favorite time there. I strolled down the allée of old plane trees to the château. Most visitors were leaving. Long shadows stretched across the path, and the arches and gallery that span the Cher River turned pink in the fading sun. At one time the château was the residence of Henry II's mistress, Diane de Poitiers. After the king's death in 1559, his widow, Catherine de Médicis, took Chenonceau for herself.

Life in the Loire Valley has not been without its dark side. There is strong fiber in a people who have endured wars, invasions, and political upheaval. During World War II this region was one of the last strongholds against the Germans. Even romantic Chenonceau played its role: as a hospital in the First World War, and for a while in the second as an escape route across the Cher, the boundary between occupied and free France. "It's over—done with," many people who were old enough to remember the painful days of World War II said to me. "Better to forget."

Jean Mangeant, who is from the Amboise area, does not forget. He tells of his father, who died while serving in the Resistance. He speaks also of events much longer ago at Amboise, and so terrible that they are seared into historical memory. Though retired now, Jean for more than 25 years guided visitors through the royal château at Amboise. On the broad ramparts today grow flowers and carefully tended lawns. Below are the steep slate roofs of the town, and beyond flows the Loire. All was not so serene in 1560. We walked into a part of the château called the King's Lodging. "Here," explained Jean Mangeant, "in retaliation for a plot against the young King François II, hundreds of Protestants were executed by hanging, drowning, decapitation. Their corpses were suspended, and left to rot, from battlements and balconies, including this one here." Estimates of the number killed vary from 250 to 1,500. "Whatever the number, the consequences were terrible," said Jean, for afterward began decades of religious wars.

Fortunately, not all the tales at Amboise are so gruesome. Jean pointed out a locked gate at one end of the rampart and a house far below. "My grandmother's house. My grandfather sold wine. A tunnel from here connects with my grandfather's cave. During World War I Amboise was used as an infirmary run by nuns. The good sisters could not understand why so many of their patients seemed so extremely happy—until they learned that my grandfather had been supplying them with wine through the tunnel!"

Amboise has another connection that intrigues Jean Mangeant, an avid bicyclist. At the invitation of François I, Leonardo da Vinci spent his last years at a manor house here called Clos Lucé, where he died in 1519. While it is not certain that Leonardo ever put the concept of a bicycle to paper, it is documented that he invented the chain gear still used to propel a bicycle.

And so, as I mounted a shiny red 12-speed, I fell right in with Loire tradition. In any case bicycling is an ideal way to tour the region. Sabina Marshall agreed. "If you wanted to go through fast, not smell the flowers or enjoy the scenery, you'd just drive through." At age 71, Sabina was the oldest of the group of two dozen bicyclists I joined for a few days. We headed from Luynes, near Tours, to a château near Chinon where the group would stay. At first the road hit some respectable hills, though for the most part the region is level. Peonies and poppies in full bloom snuggled against farmhouses that looked old enough and mossy enough to have grown right out of the earth. Frogs croaked in green ponds. Dogs barked. A farmer in his garden waved encouragingly as I struggled up one long hill. "*Vous montez!* You're climbing!" he called. I huffed a breathy *bonjour*. Scarecrows dressed in old blue work clothes seemed to flap encouragement, too.

Ilene "Iloo" Gruder, from Florida, rode along with me for a while. A trim, young-looking mother of four grown daughters, she said, "I can't see just *eating* my way through Europe!" At Langeais we left our bicycles leaning against an iron fence and crossed the drawbridge. Though austere from the outside, in contrast to many Loire châteaus that have little furniture, Langeais is carefully decorated in 15th-century style. We wandered from room to room, some lavishly appointed with carved wood chests and canopy beds. Fine Flemish tapestries covered stone walls. "To sleep in a room like this just *one* night in your life—just one night!" said Iloo. By the time we reached the royal bedchamber, where the newly wed Anne de

Bretagne and Charles VIII must have slept in December 1491, Iloo had upped her ante: "I'd like to live here for three days!"

Our biking togs were hardly appropriate for life in a château, where the 15-year-old Duchess Anne wore for her wedding a dress of cloth-of-gold, trimmed with 160 sable skins. But soon we would find a castle that would welcome us in sporty attire. We crossed the Loire from Langeais and pedaled downstream. The road, high on the levee, afforded a splendid view of the river, flowing slowly between elongated sandbars. In places poppies had turned meadows to scarlet, and buttercups riffled in the breeze like waves of gold. Behind tidy houses spread perfectly tended vegetable gardens. Water lilies floated on the placid Indre where we crossed into the village of Rigny-Ussé. Roses spilled over fences everywhere. At the far end of town rises Château d'Ussé, a tangle of turrets and towers and ramparts in soft white stone. The château may have inspired the 17th-century fairy tale "Sleeping Beauty."

A little farther downriver, the Avoine-Chinon nuclear power facility offers a sharp contrast. Dark clouds billowing in a threatening sky met the steam pouring from the plant's cooling towers in a weird futuristic twilight zone. But a couple of miles of country road brought us back into our world of fantasy at another castle fit for an enchanted princess—the Château des Réaux, a checkered, stone-and-brick structure, mirrored in a moat. One delight of the Loire region is that many châteaus and manors receive overnight guests. Each has its own unique style and flavor.

"*Bonsoir*—Good evening." Florence Goupil de Bouillé, a slender, vivacious blonde, rushed out to greet our group, wielding a master list to direct her guests to their proper rooms in her ancestral home. Then, from all over the château, came the oohs and aahs. As people found their own rooms, they then rushed to see others, up and down stairs in ancient towers to rooms tucked in at every level, each with its own charm. All the while Mme Goupil de Bouillé smiled, taking delight in the pleasure of her guests. "The experience in a private château is different. We have no telephones or room service," said Florence. At Réaux they offer much more. "My house is your house," she said. And I knew she meant it.

Upstream on the Loire, the royal château of Blois dominates the heart of a medieval city in a rich mélange of Gothic and Renaissance styles. Here in 1545 the romantic poet Pierre de Ronsard met his beloved Cassandra and found inspiration for his verse. Here also, in 1588, Henry III engineered the murder of the conspiratorial duc de Guise. On several evenings each summer local townspeople put on a "spectacle" that reviews other events of the château's rich history. As darkness falls the interior courtyard becomes a bustling medieval city. A crowd gathers, horses, goats, hounds, a donkey enter. Soon comes a clashing of broadswords, then the arrival of Jeanne d'Arc. (Yes, she was here too!) Scenes from the life of Louis XII were so convincing that one three-year-old girl near me wailed to her mother at Louis XII's demise. "*Maman, le roi est mort!* The king is dead!"

I watched with Martine Tissier de Mallerais, curator of the château. A slender woman with the fine features of a Renaissance portrait, she lives with her husband and three children in a tower of the castle. She explained the importance of the Italian Renaissance in France. "One can say that the French were beguiled by things Italian, not only by architecture, but by all sorts of things—gardens, the whole manner of life."

To the countless châteaus and grand houses we saw in the Loire, a companion had reacted: "You can see why there had to be a French Revolution."

"Yes, but that needs some explanation," Mme Tissier de Mallerais commented with a smile. "The wealth of the region did not just stay in the châteaus.

The châteaus supported artisans, those who built the châteaus, the producers of food." On Chambord alone, François I employed 1,800 men full time. Today that tradition of craftsmanship lives on in the Loire, but it is turned more to restoration of crumbling architectural treasures.

With his hand, Raymond Debenais broke a piece of tuffeau off a large block. The stone had a gray-green tinge. "It will dry hard and white," he said. "I take only the best. I live in stone, so I know it." We were at an *atelier,* or studio, where he was carving an intricate stone finial for a 15th-century house in Chinon. "The floral curves are called 'curled cabbage,' in Renaissance parlance," he said. As a sign of his status as a master sculptor Debenais wears two thin gold-wire earrings. He trained for seven years and has worked for 15 more. "You have to have gray hair to be respected," Debenais said, running a hand through salt-and-pepper curls.

Later that afternoon we visited the old house where the carving would cap the peak of the roof. And with the workmen we shared a little wine, a bottle of fruity red Chinon with a picture of François Rabelais on the label—which brought to mind the admonition: *"Beuvez tousjours; Vous ne mourrez jamais!* Drink always; you will never die!" It was altogether appropriate, for it is here in this corner of the Loire at the end of the 15th century that France's great Renaissance writer, humanist, and lover of life began his merry career. And his rollicking, bawdy satires about the pleasure-loving giants, Gargamelle and Gargantua, are set in this Chinon region. Meandering on another day, through lush pastures and vineyard-patched slopes that even a gentle spring rain could not make gloomy, I understood why Rabelais developed his appreciation of the good life here.

Upriver at Vouvray, near Tours, I visited a small vineyard called Clos du Petit-Mont. The fifth generation of his family to make wine here, Daniel Allias welcomed me and a group of wine tasters from the States. He led us into the cave, cut into the tuffeau hillside behind his house. The cave stays a constant 11 or 12 degrees Celsius, perfect for wine, a little chilly for me. Over generations the Allias family has dug out alcoves now filled with bottles covered in moldy black dust and labeled by vintage year. Deep in the cave is a little room with a fireplace. There in niches, two by two, like nesting pigeons, are stored the vineyard's most precious vintages.

Later, in the family dining room, Daniel's sister, Denise, who also helps run the vineyard, and his father joined us to sample wine. We began with a 1986; then came an '85, sweet and soft. It was serious business: first the appearance, color, clarity; then the nose, and the palate. The tasters swirled the wine around in their mouths. "This is a lovely wine," concluded one about a 1976.

For the last wine we had to guess the vintage. Daniel Allias gave us a hint: "My father made this wine. 'The father makes the wine the son drinks' goes an old French saying. I had to get a 15-day leave from the military to come home to help with the harvest. That year the spring flowering came a month early. Then a long dry summer." At last he told us, "It was 1959, a dry year with very little wine, but great wine." The wine had a mellow, honeyed taste. To all this serious talk about wine, Denise Allias lifted her glass and offered a comment Rabelais would have appreciated. "Wine, I just like to drink it!"

But what is good wine without good food? And good food is a way of life in the Loire. The first essential, good fresh ingredients, abounds here: luscious fruits and vegetables, fresh fish from the Loire, mushrooms, goat cheeses—the list goes on. Time is important too, to savor meals that may last two or three hours. And good cooks, they're vital. It is a tradition that Christel Debat-Cauvin continues in the valley of the Manse near Saint-Épain. "If you like to eat, you will be a good cook. And if you like to eat, you will like life and love—it all goes together," she said, plunging her hands into dough for honey bread. For the last four years she and her husband have worked nonstop, restoring and running their hostelry in the old orangery and servants' quarters of the Château de Montgoger, which was burned out a hundred years ago. Surrounded by forest, the ruined, overgrown mansion looms hauntingly nearby, like some relic of Sherman's march through Georgia. It's tranquil here. The only sound I ever heard in the mornings was a cuckoo calling repeatedly, like a Swiss clock gone berserk.

Mme Debat-Cauvin stirred up a pot of crab shells bubbling on the stove, stock for a delicate crab mousseline. "It's a lot of trouble to make!" she said with a laugh. She and her husband used to have a restaurant in Paris. But now she loves the Loire. With the conviction of the converted, she insists "I'll *never* go back to Paris!"

Presentation is important in a good meal, too. At a well-known restaurant in Amboise, lunch came at a leisurely pace—delicate hors d'oeuvres, then my main course of *sandre,* a perch-like fish from the Loire, with lobster sauce. My friends had chosen duck. I wondered why I had china different from theirs, until I looked a little closer. The bright flower pattern on my plate was actually made of sauces, carefully, intricately swirled into exquisite little yellow, orange, and green blossoms!

Even the plainest eatery can have style: for instance the place where I had lunch in Fontevraud—the ancient abbey town where Richard Cœur de Lion and Eleanor of Aquitaine are laid to rest. It was an unpretentious *brasserie* where roof workers restoring the slate on the old abbey were eating. My simple salad arrived, crowned with a perfect red rose made from a tomato peel.

There is a pride in the individuals who produce the foods in this region. Often the chef may bid you good-bye after your meal—wearily, if it is late, with his *toque,* or chef's cap, a little wilted, but proud of having provided a worthy repast. At their goat farm near Sainte-Maure-de-Touraine, to the east of Chinon, Marie-Madeleine and Armand LeBoeuf take pride, too, in the *chèvre,* or goat cheese, they produce. Baaing softly, 80 or 90 russet-colored nannies nuzzled around us in a large paddock. One happily nibbled my slacks leg to see if khaki was to her liking. "They are very curious and very affectionate," said Marie-Madeleine. With goats there are no holidays, milking twice a day. "And when you are finished that, you have to make the cheese," said Marie-Madeleine, showing me how the milk is processed. And then, of course, she came in with a tray of bread and cheese—"It's to your taste?" she asked, watching as I downed my fourth piece of the delicate, fresh cheese.

Late on another day I watched a small red balloon waft tentatively, then soar swiftly upward into a brightening sky. "I told you it would clear. You didn't believe me?" said Michel Bergounioux. The Frenchman carefully studied the drift of the trial balloon, took a compass reading, then said firmly, "We'll fly south, so we head north to take off. Let's go!" We climbed into a van and sped north. By now I was a believer. A steady downpour and sullen skies had lasted most of the day, but had cleared as if by magic in the afternoon. I had joined a group of people touring the Loire Valley by hot-air balloon. When we reached the Château de Gizeux, a private estate where we had permission to take off, we spread two enormous flowered balloons out on the grass. Big fans blew air into the shapeless fabric, which slowly began to fill and rise.

I clambered into one of the wicker gondolas, along with four other passengers, who were from Mexico City, and pilot Michel. Attired in a blue blazer, tie, and deerstalker hat to complement his handlebar mustache, Michel was ready to go. He fired up the propane burners. The huge balloons became taut with the hot air and reached their full nine-story height. Then gently, without any sensation of movement, we lifted. The sprawling château shrinking quickly beneath us gave the only indication of how swiftly we ascended. The breeze swept us rapidly away across large, carefully groomed forests, and over pastures where cows started at our appearance. Michel cut the burners, and we floated in silence, enraptured by the scene below. A counterpane of fields, yellow and green, tidily edged by rows of trees and hedges, spread to the horizon, with farmsteads and châteaus sheltered in groves of trees. "There must be 10,000 châteaus in France," he remarked.

"We go north, and I want to go south!" said Michel, slightly perturbed at a wind shift. "The same thing happened yesterday!" Below, the van with our ground crew raced to keep up with us. "Near the ground I am in control on the centimeter," he added. It was no boast. He cut the burners and we dropped to young pines and oaks, brushing the top branches. Then we descended even lower over a marsh. Two ducks made a fast getaway, and a muskrat splashed under the water. We swished through soft grass and reeds with an exhilarating sense of speed. Below we could see our faces mirrored in the water. To get us over a row of trees fast approaching, Michel fired up the burners.

Ballooning in France comes out of a long tradition. The first flight of a manned hot-air balloon—or *Montgolfière,* as the French call it in honor of the brothers whose experiments led to that voyage—soared over Paris on November 21, 1783. How Michel got hooked on ballooning belongs in a French farce. "It was about 15 years ago," as he tells the story, "the first time I saw a balloon. It was over my house. I jumped into my car and chased it. Another car was doing the same thing. We collided. Totaled both vehicles." But he set about the next day to learn ballooning.

Michel gallantly tipped his hat as we drifted over houses where farmers and their families waved. The burners glowed brightly in the diminishing light of the setting sun, offering a welcome warmth in the chill air. Soon we would have to land. Michel signaled to the crew below, followed now by a trail of cars. With a skilled maneuver of ropes and flaps, we touched down, pitched slightly into a cornfield and stopped, as the crew, along with a team of local men, women, and children, wrestled the huge balloon to the ground. Out came a small table, a cloth, glasses, chilled champagne and wine, soft drinks. Toasts and libations and thanks flew all around to our impromptu landing crew. To questions about what ballooning was like, *"Fantastique!"* seemed an adequate and easily understood reply.

Michel introduced us all: Four Mexicans, one American, two English. . . . "Aha," broke in one bearded young farmer in the crowd, looking at our British crew with a broad grin: "You're the ones who burned Jeanne d'Arc. We got rid of you!" Memories run deep in the Loire country.

And so does kindness. Our group accepted the offer of Daniel and Rolande Lebeu to visit their home in the nearby village of Channay-sur-Lathan. In a warm kitchen, Rolande washed and dried delicate colored wine glasses and set them on a table that nearly filled the room. She passed tea cookies. Daniel brought out a bottle of Vouvray from his brother-in-law's vineyard. The fresh, light wine went down easily. Out came another bottle. Daniel would have offered us wine all night, but we finally had to leave. "We are simple people," he said, raising his glass to us, "but when I have a friend at my table, everything I have is for him."

"A diamond . . . with the Indre for a setting"—so the French writer Honoré de Balzac described Azay-le-Rideau. This 16th-century château now comes to life each summer as actors relive its history. Costumed in Renaissance dress, cast members relax at river's edge.

Boxwood and yew shape intricate pathways in the Garden of Love (left) at Château de Villandry. Though less romantic in motif, vegetable beds (above) make a colorful array of geometric designs. The gardens at Villandry, although built in this century, reflect 16th-century styles. A thousand years earlier, the Loire Valley already was producing fine fruits and wines. A golden-hued Vouvray (right), vintage 1931, continues that tradition.

FOLLOWING PAGES: Spring poppies entice a stroller in the Loire, often called the Garden of France.

I n the cool of evening, hot-air balloons drift across the Vienne River toward Chinon, spread below the protective walls of its formidable fortress-castle. Two other 90-foot-tall balloons (right) prepare for takeoff at Gizeux, one of many private châteaus in the Loire. With a tug on a line, veteran pilot Michel Bergounioux (opposite) maneuvers his craft. Pioneered over Paris two centuries ago, hot-air ballooning today provides a popular way to view the gently rolling landscape of the Loire Valley.

EUROPE

"At last—for the first time—I live!" proclaimed the American writer Henry James upon reaching Rome. He journeyed there in the 19th century, during the latter days of the era of the grand tour. Italy was often the ultimate goal of travelers in Europe then. It was France, however, that particularly entranced Thomas Jefferson the century before. He wrote in 1787: "From Lyons to Nismes I have been nourished with the remains of Roman grandeur." Americans have long been drawn to Europe, for from there comes much of our political and cultural identity.

Though today's modern transportation brings near the farthest, most exotic corners of the earth, the allure of Europe does not diminish. The gentle pleasures of the Loire Valley that I enjoyed—the pastoral terrain, the châteaus and medieval cities, the agreeable life-style—are only a small part of the reward Europe offers. Throughout the continent there are sumptuous palaces, museums of priceless treasures, glorious basilicas and cathedrals, classic temples and amphitheaters that offer a vision of a splendid past. The attraction of Europe comes also in roaming ancient villages and walled towns where the patina of centuries lends a softness and warmth rarely found in the newness of America. Or of sipping coffee in a café and observing the daily bustle, going on just as it must have for the past several hundred years.

In Europe—the smallest continent except for Australia—live about a sixth of the world's people, with a proliferation of cultures and languages. Here are more than 30 nations—territories that vary in size from tiny Vatican City to the enormous European U.S.S.R. Across this sweeping expanse between the Atlantic Ocean and the Ural Mountains is a profusion of natural delights: Ireland's emerald countryside, the Portuguese Algarve, the French Dordogne, the snowcapped Alps, Greek isles set in azure seas, the craggy Dalmatian coast, Scandinavia's land of the midnight sun.

For Americans, part of the appeal of Europe is, in a sense, one of the *familiar*. Even without ever visiting the continent, we have, from childhood on, already been there in a way. And we have our images: the turreted castles of Sleeping Beauty . . . the dark, haunting forest of Hansel and Gretel. We know Romeo and Juliet's Verona, and Chaucer's Canterbury.

There is another kind of familiarity here, too. The ancestral roots of many of us lie in Europe. Perhaps even a village or a castle will carry a surname. Several years ago in the Scottish highlands, on a heathery, windswept knoll, I looked down on a crumbling castle that bore my family name. Broodingly beautiful at the edge of a lake, it evoked a world of clansmen, kings, and ancient wars. My ancestors probably had no real tie to the place, but somehow the name lent a personal link. Whether one emerged from a crofter's cot or a grand palace, the romance of Europe often comes in peering through the long telescope of time. —*Jennifer C. Urquhart*

Elaborate turrets soar in an architectural flight of fancy—Bavaria's Neuschwanstein Castle. Built in the 19th century in medieval style, the fairy-tale palace in southeastern Germany fulfilled the romantic vision of Wittelsbach's "Mad King" Ludwig II.

THE TIROL
Austria

Wreathed in clouds, the Zugspitze bulks immense over a village in the Austrian Tirol.
Cable cars give access to the peak of the 9,721-foot mountain — West Germany's
highest. From there, visitors can survey the Austrian, Bavarian, and Swiss Alps.

45

NORTHERN WATERS
Norway

Waters of Strynevatnet Lake mirror Fosnes, a remote dairy village in a corner of western Norway. Friaren waterfall (right), whose name in English means "the suitor," tumbles down rocky stairsteps at nearby Geirangerfjorden—one of the most-visited of the steep-walled sea inlets that breach Norway's coastal mountains.

BRUGGE
Belgium

Fourteenth-century stone bridge arches over a canal in the Belgian city of Brugge, named for its many bridges. Ornately facaded buildings below—where today cafés and restaurants spill into the Grote Markt, the great marketplace—once housed trade guilds.

FOLLOWING PAGES: Mist softens one of Belgium's oldest canals, linking Brugge with Gent 25 miles away. Such waters provide an ideal route for commerce—and for leisurely boating.

CAROLINE SHEEN; MICHAEL S. YAMASHITA (RIGHT AND FOLLOWING PAGES)

VENICE
Italy

Gondolier threads a narrow canal in Venice, venerable city on the Adriatic. Motorboats now ply some canals, but gondolas, bobbing at left, still afford serene transport. Built in a lagoon on more than a hundred small islands, Venice reflects a blend of Byzantine East and Renaissance West. For centuries, the city reigned as an independent republic and a world trading power. The legacy of that time lives on in the lavish palaces and grand churches that seem adrift on Venice's waterways.

Paris by night shimmers with images that have made the city synonymous with romance. The couple below shares a moment on a bridge over the Seine River, which arcs through the heart of France's capital. Symbol of Paris, the Eiffel Tower (right) sweeps skyward. Built for the international exhibition of 1889, the steel tower draws more than four million visitors a year. From its thousand-foot height, viewers look out over the city that has enthralled poets, painters, and other artists—as well as travelers from the world over.

RONNIE KAUFMAN/THE STOCK MARKET; AL ASSID/THE STOCK MARKET (RIGHT)

THE EAST

BHUTAN

By Cynthia Russ Ramsay
Photographs by Paul Chesley

F ar away, sequestered in the eastern reaches of the mighty Himalayas, the long-forbidden kingdom of Bhutan was virtually sealed off from the rest of the world for centuries. Until just a few years ago, time stood still, preserving a medieval society in which monks had a monopoly on learning, serfs raised what was needed on feudal estates, and everyone worried a lot about demons and evil spirits.

As recently as 1961 there were no cities, no telephones, newspapers, post offices, or cinemas. No one had a car, not even the monarch, because roads did not exist. Taxes were paid in kind—rice, cheese, or cloth—and barter was the usual form of trade. The government did not begin issuing printed money until the late 1960s.

When Father Mackey arrived in 1963, he was able to live for three weeks on a bag of salt, exchanging a few ounces at a time for eggs, potatoes, or rice. A Canadian-born Jesuit, he came in response to a royal invitation to help set up the present system of high schools in the country. Until that time, fewer than a hundred Westerners had gained admission to Bhutan.

Natural barriers reinforced the government's policy of isolation, and the difficult terrain along the borders helped keep people out. Only mule tracks penetrated the jungle on the frontier with India. In the north, precipitous passes through the snowy ramparts of the Himalayas offered only slow, arduous access from Tibet.

Today, even though the kingdom has cautiously opened its doors to the 20th century, life for nearly all of the estimated 1.3 million people still goes on much as it did in decades past. Even now, as new motor roads and limited air service link Bhutan to the rest of the world, the number of foreign visitors is strictly limited. The Switzerland-size nation remains somehow different, somehow special, beckoning the traveler with the enchantment of the remote, the barely attainable.

Bhutan is a place where fortress-like castles house government offices; where masked dancers drive away demons; soothsayers reside on army bases; and high civilian officials wear three-foot-long swords. In the most recent development plan, preserving the age-old culture is considered as important as building factories.

His Majesty Jigme Singye Wangchuck, a handsome, athletic 32-year-old, tells visitors, "The blessings of our traditions must be balanced against the benefits of technology. We do not want to sacrifice our spiritual strength for an increase in production. Our standard of living won't improve, if we let modernization destroy our values and our way of life." The young monarch always appears in the distinctive national dress—a knee-length, kimono-like *kho,* worn by nobles as well as by farmers.

Twin-engine planes have made regular flights to Bhutan from India since 1983 and from Bangladesh since 1986. They take off only if visibility is near perfect

In festival finery, a teenager stands beneath a fresco of a tiger inside the fortress-like dzong *in the village of Tongsa. The Bhutanese create such ferocious beasts to guard the castle-monasteries, which serve as local religious and administrative centers in the land of the Thunder Dragon.*

for skimming over high ridges. If the fickle mountain weather suddenly spawns too many clouds, the planes turn back. During the last 30 minutes of my nearly two-hour flight from Calcutta, I could see the fabled snow-covered giants in the distance, along the Tibetan border—pure white and as ethereal as a dream. Below us, so close one might think we were driving, waterfalls foamed through dense evergreen forests. Wooded peaks, ascending above 12,000 feet, rose sheer over terraced fields. The rumpled jade landscape is part of a series of north-south ranges that separate the country into the high valleys where most Bhutanese live.

Descending rapidly, the plane banked into the Paro Valley, lying at almost 7,800 feet, and we touched down on a runway set in the midst of small plots of young, green wheat. At last I was in the home of the Thunder Dragon, or *Druk-kyul*—the inhabitants' name for a land of rumbling mountain storms. Dominating the neatly tilled Paro Valley was a towering white citadel with massive walls that sloped slightly inward, so that the great structure seemed to grow out of the ground. A religious and administrative center, called a *dzong,* its outlines were simpler and more austere than those of a European castle, but it had a striking grandeur that made me wonder what mysteries it guarded.

Scattered on hillsides and fields were three-story, whitewashed farmhouses with low-pitched, shingled roofs—each pine slat anchored against the winds by a white stone. From a distance the homes looked like alpine chalets, except for the narrow, arched windows framed in wood painted with colorful designs. Here and there on high ridges and knolls, white pennants gleamed in halos of sunlight. The Bhutanese believe that every flutter of these prayer flags, which are imprinted with sacred Buddhist incantations, sends forth their blessings and brings merit to those who planted them. Other monuments of the Buddhist faith caught my eye. These were wayside shrines, called *chortens.* Like small houses without windows or doors, most are whitewashed and painted all around with horizontal red bands. Together, these various structures gave a distinct Bhutanese look to the landscape.

Apart from the airport and the road, the view had changed little from what the first Europeans—two Portuguese Jesuits—saw in 1627. A journal of their trip describes the same sprawling town with houses that "do not line up to the streets . . . the high buildings greatly beautified by windows and verandahs . . . and many irrigation canals."

The 17th century and a simple, nearly self-sufficient agrarian life were never far away during my journey through the mountainous heart of Bhutan, where 95 percent of the population earn a living as farmers and herders. Even the burgeoning capital, Thimphu, was making only a tentative accommodation to modern times.

Thimphu was my first stop on the east-west highway—a narrow, tortuous route twisting around one mountain after another. Distances on the corkscrew road have to be measured in time—not in miles. It took my able driver, Lobzang Dakpa, $1\frac{1}{2}$ hours to cover the 37 miles from Paro east to Thimphu. Signs direct drivers to honk before negotiating each hairpin turn. Sometimes just inches separate a vehicle from a ravine hundreds of feet deep.

There was little traffic—a bus crammed with smiling passengers, an occasional car, and a few trucks, wonderfully gaudy with vivid decorations painted on everything but the windshield. Pedestrians were in far greater evidence, many bent beneath burdens of firewood, sacks of rice, and bundles of other produce. The women carried as much as the men, unless they had a child tied on the back with a shawl.

Like the fictional Shangri-La, mountainous Bhutan long existed in isolation. In 1962
a paved road linked the nation to India. In this Himalayan realm, about the size of
Switzerland, terrain ranges from lofty peaks of perpetual snow to semitropical lowland jungle.

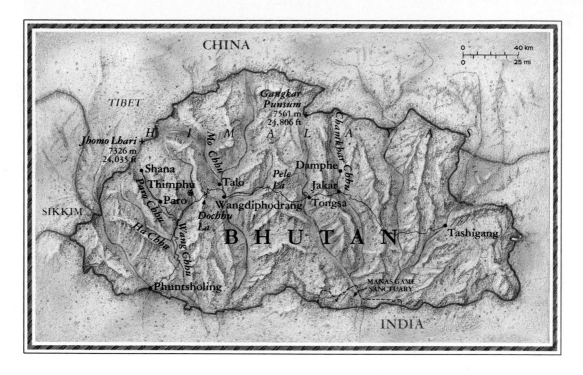

Afternoon clouds were beginning to coalesce and swallow the high ridges by the time we wriggled around a steep slope and looked down upon the Thimphu Valley to the town built on the banks of the Wang Chhu. (*Chhu* is the word for river.) In the distance, a large bell-shaped memorial to the late king glowed like an ember, as a shaft of sunlight fired its gilded dome. The flash of gold also embellished the Tashichho Dzong, where small pagoda-like towers surmounted the broad red roofs.

Close up, the scene in town contained child monks in maroon robes, with cheeks as red as radishes, archers practicing the national sport, and a single main street of gaily painted storefronts. For sale were such imports as radios, tennis shoes, and soap powder, but generally the selection of consumer goods was limited. Not so the supply of *chang,* a popular, slightly sour barley beer sold at open-fronted establishments. At the two main intersections, a traffic policeman signaled nonexistent traffic to halt as he waved us on. A pagoda roof and carved posts lent character to the gas station, and if the fictional Shangri-La had had cars, petrol would have been sold in a place just like this.

As a town, Thimphu sprang into being in the early 1960s, when the late king embarked on his plan to modernize Bhutan and make this his capital. "Just five years ago there were rice fields and pine forests where we have houses and offices," said Dago Beda, urbane and businesslike manager of the Bhutan Tourist Corporation. Like all government officials she spoke excellent English as well as Dzongkha, the national language.

I had stopped at the tourist office to arrange my itinerary. Travel in Bhutan is tightly controlled, and tourists do not move around the country on their own. They are generally restricted to package tours, accompanied by a local guide, for the government is determined to avoid the disruptive effects of mass tourism.

A scant 2,400 came in 1987, and there are no plans to increase the numbers. "We want to keep our religious ceremonies sacred and to avoid turning them into tourist events," said Dago with a crisp smile.

I chanced upon just such a Buddhist ritual at Thimphu's dzong—site of the National Assembly, summer residence of the head abbot, the spiritual leader of the country, and scene of esoteric ceremonies in temples crowded with gods. With Françoise Pommaret-Imaeda, a French scholar in her 30s, I strolled across an inner courtyard surrounded by the dzong's complex of buildings. At the main temple the entire facade was given over to a series of wall paintings in vivid colors. We stopped before the Wheel of Life, one of the major themes of Bhutanese art. It portrayed the realms of rebirth with images drawn to rules precisely defined in scriptures. Complex and detailed as a tapestry, the mural illustrated what every Bhutanese knows—only on earth, which has the teachings of Buddha, can one escape the cycle of rebirths, find enlightenment, and attain the blissful state of nirvana.

As I studied the work, the sounds of chanting, deep and sonorous like the distant rumble of thunder, came from within the temple. Stepping out of our shoes, we entered a sumptuous chamber whose dim interior gleamed with color. There were so many things to see. Innumerable meticulous paintings of divine figures covered the walls, ceiling, and wooden pillars. Dozens of butter lamps in silver bowls glowed before an altar crowded with votive offerings, peacock feathers, and incense. Just behind stood a gilded statue, radiant in the wavering light.

"He is Padmasambhava, the missionary also known as Guru Rimpoche—'Precious Teacher.' In the eighth century he spread the teachings of Buddha throughout the Himalayas," whispered Françoise. I was to hear of this saint many times, for he is a great spiritual force in Bhutan, venerated in temples, celebrated in legends, and honored at festivals.

At a distance from the altar, monks sat cross-legged, shoulder-to-shoulder in two facing rows, rocking back and forth to the rapid rhythm of their prayers. We were witnessing part of a funeral ceremony. The monks were reciting from texts that guide the soul through *Bardo* on its way to its next existence. In this limbo, which lasts for 49 days, the soul encounters all sorts of terrifying deities. These prayers remind the spirit of the Buddhist belief that all phenomena of existence, such as these monsters, are mere shadows and illusions.

My mind wandered to another day, when I had heard one of Himalayan Buddhism's most revered teachers speak of illusion and reality. "Take, for example, a cup of water," Khyengtse Rimpoche had said. "For you, it is something to drink. But if you put a fish in the cup, it will see water as a place to live. The Buddha will see neither liquid nor a home; he will see the true nature of existence behind the temporary combination of atoms. This reality cannot be expressed in words. It's like a mute eating candy; he knows the taste of sweetness, but cannot express it."

A booming drumbeat silenced the prayers for the dead, and there followed an interval of melancholy music played by five monks who stared impassively ahead throughout the performance. A low-pitched trumpet moaned; cymbals clashed; a small bell trilled sharp, brassy sounds, and the single hand-held drum set a slow, stark rhythm.

Then the chorus began again, intoning in hollow voices from texts written in Choekey, the canonical language of Tibet and the equivalent of Latin in Bhutanese scriptures. The use of Choekey is one of the many instances of the strong cultural and religious ties to Tibet; before the border was closed in 1959, the brightest Bhutanese monks regularly went there for higher theological studies. Today, they may go to

Phajoding, a *gompa,* or monastery, perched astride a 12,000-foot ridge, about a mile directly above Thimphu.

From my hotel window, I had wondered about the cluster of white buildings grazing the sky. Like Oz, Phajoding seemed impossibly remote and celestial. "We will go there tomorrow," said Wangchuk Wangdi, an instinctive philosopher as well as a farmer, an entrepreneur, and a tourist guide. His strong Mongol features were accented by his drooping mustache, and his almond-shaped eyes betrayed an intelligence and humor that eased the four sweaty hours on the trail. Born on a farm in the Ha Valley 35 years ago, Wangchuk remembers when public education arrived in the country. His opportunity for learning came when a government official showed up to select a few students for the new regional primary school. "Our landlord offered my mother a bonus if she would supply someone to take his son's place," said Wangchuk. "In those days parents bribed the recruiters to keep children home to work on the farm; now the problem is meeting the demand for education."

At first the trail followed the river, which tumbled through pine forests with a soft, unceasing song. Dainty Himalayan sparrows twittered a more staccato melody. "They are singing encouragement to us," said Wangchuk. "I hear them saying it's very beautiful here. Come up. Come up."

From time to time, Wangchuk stopped to put a betel leaf neatly wrapped around an areca nut into his mouth. This astringent chew, called *doma,* is far more common here than cigarettes are in the United States. "In the old days, even two enemies plotting to kill each other had to exchange doma if they met."

As we climbed higher, the river vanished into another fold of the mountain, and the path grew steeper. We entered a spruce landscape jeweled with scarlet rhododendrons and draped with lichens, which filtered the sunlight so it hung in the trees like soft mist.

P hajoding! We could see the buildings and their array of prayer flags every step of the way. We had left the spruce forest behind and entered the zone of juniper scrub, grasses, and rhododendrons. Even the clouds seemed close. "Maybe we will reach them at the gompa and can ride them back down to Thimphu," sighed Wangchuk.

As we finally arrived, a bell rang sharply in the thin air, sending the 73 seminarians to their rooms for solitary study; among them was 21-year-old Gyeltsen. (Some Bhutanese use only one name.) Four years ago Gyeltsen had been selected from the Paro Dzong, where his parents had enrolled him when he was barely five. "In the past, one son was always sent to the monastery," said Wangchuk. "Parents still feel it's good to have a monk in the family—someone who can be relied upon to pray and perform ceremonies in their behalf."

Gyeltsen has never read anything but religious books—nor does he want to. It will take him another ten years or so to complete his studies. During that time he will go into retreat for the prescribed three years, three months, and three days. "I will have more time for meditation, which calms the mind," he said. "To calm a flame, you place a glass around it. Meditation is like that glass."

Speaking to Wangchuk in Dzongkha, Gyeltsen invited us into his room. Almost immediately he served us tea with milk and a bowl of the popular snack called *zao,* a puffed rice that had been soaked in water and baked. The room contained a small painted chest, bedding folded in the corner, and an altar covered by a red curtain. A small, low table with a few religious texts—long, narrow pages bound between two wooden boards—completed the furnishings. Strips of dried yak meat hung from the rafters. Glass in the arched windows, instead of the traditional wooden shutters, blocked the cold wind and provided a view of alpine meadows, where shaggy yaks were silhouetted against the sky. A small kerosene stove for cooking was the only modern convenience. For a bath, which was outdoors, the monks heated stones and dropped them into a wooden tub half filled with water.

Normally, monks receive all their education in a monastery, take their vows of celibacy at 14, and are fully ordained at 20. Recently about 20 out of a total of some 200 graduates of the public school system turned their backs on promising careers for the rewards of a monastic life. Passang, a slender young man with a full round face and a sweet smile, was a monk of this exceptional breed. He entered the room with a slight bow. In hesitant English, he explained he had decided in the fifth grade to become a monk but had waited because he wanted to gain knowledge of the outside world. He had to work extra hard because his secular education had given him no training in Choekey and no experience with the rote system of learning.

"Here we must learn so many pages by heart every day," he said, redraping the toga-like folds of his robe over one shoulder. "For our examinations the masters will recite a line from the scriptures, and we must say what follows."

Unlike most of the other monks, Passang believes the earth is round. I asked him how he reconciled the astronomy taught in the public schools with the cosmic diagrams in the temples, which show Mount Meru in the center of a flat universe. "We see Meru and such things with a special eye," he replied.

Detached from the world in their aerie, the gentle, pious young ascetics do, indeed, view the world through the lens of a deep, unwavering Buddhist faith.

"That fervor brings a peace and contentment, which can be a tremendous weapon against disease," said Pema Dorji, prominent doctor of indigenous medicine at a hospital in Thimphu. "All the time we are treating patients, we recite mantras (short magical prayers). They make the medicine more potent," he said, pausing as Wangchuk translated his words.

Old Tibetan texts refer to Bhutan as the land of sweet-scented, medicinal herbs. Plants collected in the mountains and the tropical lowlands are still used by local doctors, who have a wealth of knowledge about nature's remedies. Pema Dorji and his colleagues attend more than 55,000 patients a year, and in Thimphu I heard several testimonials to their cures.

"Some roots and leaves must be dried in the sun; others require shade," Pema Dorji said, as he ushered me through a room lined with shelves of labeled apothecary jars. He opened some airtight containers, and I caught a whiff of cloves—beneficial to the heart; cardamom for the stomach and liver; and garlic for the blood.

Many Bhutanese blame evil spirits for their ills and turn to exorcists for treatment. "I've seen it work," exclaimed Father Mackey, now Chief Inspector of Schools. "When I was teaching in Tashigang, in the east, I watched a lama wind a ball of twine around a patient's entire body. There followed an elaborate three-hour ceremony, with prayers, music, and holy water, to drive the demons into the space enclosed by the twine," said Father Mackey. "Then the lama cut the twine, put it in a box, burned it, and threw the ashes in the river. Afterwards, the patient stepped back and forth over a dish of live coals. The man had been bedridden for weeks, but he was up and around the next day! These people have tremendous faith in a supreme spiritual power much greater than themselves, greater than any lama's, yet manifested and channeled through the lama."

After more than two decades of life and labor in Bhutan, Father Mackey, a tall, vigorous 72, wouldn't live anywhere else. "When I am away, I miss the friendliness. When you arrive in a village, people show a real interest in you. Here you are an individual."

He also admires the egalitarian nature of the society. "Sure there was a feudal system until 1959. But the serfs were part of the family, with the same food and clothing. When the first king of the present Wangchuck dynasty started a small school at court, the children of his servants went to class with the royal heir. Some of those students have become leaders of the country."

On the following day, I set out from Thimphu for the Bumthang district in central Bhutan, a region out-of-bounds for tourists until 1982. The car carried camping gear, provisions for a trek we planned up the Chamkhar Valley, and two new passengers—Yeshey, gregarious mountaineer and guide, and Tegala, our cook, whose singing voice compensated for his culinary shortcomings. Beyond the guarded checkpoint, where an official examined my permit to travel east of Thimphu, the car climbed steadily to Dochhu La, a 10,000-foot mountain pass, which on a clear day provides a vista of the high Himalayas.

Wisps of mist, like the breath of some giant beast, straggled across the forested slopes. Scudding clouds, dark and heavy, cast deep shadows that turned the spruce a somber black. Only the profusion of purple flowers along the road lent a cheerful note to the landscape, made melancholy by the weather.

Prayer flags snapped in the raw wind as we stepped out at the pass and scanned the sky. For a magical moment, the clouds drew apart, and we caught a glimpse of Gangkar Punsum, some 25,000 feet high in the distance. The summit, incandescent in a slanting beam of sunlight, seemed to float on a sea of clouds, mysterious rather than overpowering.

The two or three attempts to scale the peak had failed, and recently the government closed the door to all further expeditions. "It's more appealing to gaze at a mountain that has never felt the foot of man," said Yeshey, voicing the official policy and that unique Bhutanese predilection for keeping the world at bay.

The road coiled down to terraced farms and the town of Wangdiphodrang. Its dzong stood on a spur of land several hundred feet above the confluence of the Mo Chhu and the Wang Chhu—the bold lines of the bastion somehow in perfect harmony with its setting. Like most of the great dzongs, it traces its origins back to the 17th century, when Shabdrung Ngawang Namgyal entered Bhutan from Tibet and united the country for the first time.

Before passing through the dzong's massive wooden doors, Yeshey draped a white sash over one shoulder, as custom requires. Inside, we walked past the civil offices to the monastery to visit Yeshey's brother-in-law, Sangay Tshering. A solemn, strapping monk in his 30s, he broke into a warm smile when I brought out a Polaroid camera. Hastily, he removed his sandals and put on embroidered felt boots before posing for me in full regalia. Otherwise, our visit did not interfere with the routine. The young novices, sitting cross-legged in the gallery around the yard, looked up only briefly and then resumed their chanting as they memorized prayers by reading them aloud, again and again. By the time they are ordained, some monks specialize in making *tormas,* painted votive cakes of butter and flour. Others play music, perform in sacred dances, or specialize in astrology. Sangay was the monastery's disciplinarian, monitoring the youngsters in the way they sit, walk, wear their robes, perform ceremonies, and generally behave.

Our destination that evening was the government guest house at Tongsa, six hours away on the road that carried us up into the clouds at the lofty pass called Pele La—the boundary between western and central Bhutan. My brief stay in Tongsa began by candlelight, for electricity had not yet reached the small town, though it was on the way. Before I departed, I encountered a spectacle of dance and color that gave Tongsa a brightness of its own.

To the accompaniment of trumpets and drums, monk dancers in voluminous brocade skirts, wide-sleeved robes, and broad-brimmed hats whirled in the courtyard of the local dzong. Scarves attached to their capes and hats fanned around them in arcs of color. Though the repetition of the stately, measured steps made the Black Hat Dance look somewhat simple, every movement had been carefully codified and choreographed in the scriptures. Even the gestures of the hands had ritual significance, for I was watching not only an artistic ballet but also a sacred rite to expel evil from the community and protect the Tongsa Valley. In other dances, monks wearing masks with ferocious fangs and bulging eyes impersonated gods and goddesses in the terrifying forms they assume to combat demons.

Two hours from Tongsa, in the village of Jakar, Tegala, the cook, loaded packhorses for our trek with tents, pots, food, and bottled drinking water purchased especially for me. In the meantime, I strolled through the small bazaar. Two yak herders, who had walked three days from their camp above 12,000 feet, were buying rice, chilies, and tea—the staples of the Bhutanese diet. In a tea shop, a saucy red-cheeked waitress flirted with her customers, but Yeshey wouldn't translate their lively repartee. A child monk smiled shyly at me. I offered him a cookie, and he reached into the folds of his robe and offered me a sour ball candy.

No one wandered the streets hungry, begging, or looking for work. The typical Bhutanese family owns a house, cattle, and land. Per capita income is less than $200 a year, but I would characterize the life-style as one of simplicity rather than poverty. As Irish travel writer Dervla Murphy points out, "poverty denotes a lack of necessities and simplicity a lack of needs."

Although work can be hard and conditions primitive, the people have a hearty enjoyment of life. Take the village of Damphe, a five-hour walk up the Chamkhar Valley from Jakar. There was much chattering and joking in the fields, where the women toiled alongside the men, spreading fertilizer on land tilled by bullock-drawn plows. From the forests that rose steeply above the young wheat and newly planted potatoes came other villagers with firewood. Nearly bent double under their loads, they smiled and greeted us when they passed. "Where did we come from; where were we going?" they wanted to know. One little girl of four, maybe five, named Deki, was carrying about 25 pounds.

That evening, when moonlight turned the white blossoms on the pear trees to silver, we visited a local farmhouse. As I climbed the notched-log ladder from the cattle barn on the ground floor, I could hear voices raised in song and laughter. In the large living area, dimly lit by candles, six girls were dancing in a semicircle, stepping from side to side, with arms linked around each other's waists. Several men, not all of them young, soon joined them.

"Our custom is to offer you a drink, whether you take it or not," said Kesang, our hostess, greeting me with a cup of barley beer. More people drifted in. The chorus became louder, the mood merrier.

In their high valleys, surrounded by steep, wild mountains, the Bhutanese find joy in their friendships, strong family ties, and deeply felt faith. During much of my stay, I had been drawn to the living landscape, and to the dignified, sociable people who still inhabit an unmechanized world in an uncommercialized way. But Bhutan is also a land of grand scenery. In the tropical southern foothills, a menagerie of wild beasts—tigers, elephants, rhinos, golden langur monkeys, and deer—wander at will in the Manas Game Sanctuary.

To the far north, the tremendous creations of the high Himalayas soar above the clouds. Here melting glaciers surge into tumultuous rivers, winds shriek in the vast silences, and the rare and elusive snow leopard prowls the crags, stalking the blue sheep. Only the seminomadic yak herders dwell in the presence of these spectacular heights, for the lesser mountains, rising to 12,000-15,000 feet, wall off the narrow valleys and block the giants from view.

The most accessible route to the high-altitude world of white peaks and yak pastures follows the Paro Chhu. For three days we trekked along the river, which foamed and swirled over huge boulders. Our destination was the camp at the base of Jhomo Lhari, a massive pyramid that soars more than 24,000 feet.

On the first day, the trail skirted the village of Shana, where children, playing with great bouquets of rhododendrons, greeted us with laughter. We passed an aged couple heading for Paro in a litany of prayer. She murmured as she fingered her prayer beads. He whirled a small hand-held prayer wheel as he walked, chanting *"Om mani padme hum*—Om, the jewel in the lotus"—the mystical invocation that resounds throughout the Himalayas.

In higher country, the scenery became bolder, and the valleys opened out to the sky, grazed by jagged peaks. Great rocky escarpments, veined with snow, gave majestic proportions to the forests and meadows. Glaciers glistened in cirques. Waterfalls were frozen into icefalls. A small shrine marked the end of one steep stretch of trail. Beside the chorten, travelers had placed boughs of spruce, saying, as one of our guides explained, *"Lha Gye Lo*—let God be the winner."

The third day of our trek took us above 12,000 feet to the domain of the yak herders. "We don't move the herds up to summer pastures until June," said Nima, mother of seven. Knitting as she talked, Nima told me she stays behind at this permanent winter settlement to raise turnips, potatoes, and radishes during the summer months. Otherwise, the yak is the mainstay of their lives—the source of meat, cheese, and butter for food and trade; hair for a coarse cloth; and dung for fuel and fertilizer. Nima's household owned a hundred yaks, each named at birth. Of course, she could identify every single one, she said, motioning me to drink my tea.

Ahead of us was Jhomo Lhari, but heavy, gray clouds and swirling mists stole the view. Snow began to fall in tiny round flakes, descending like a gauze curtain. Shapes loomed as shadows, and the only color was the fire, where Tegala was brewing tea. The cookhouse was a half-enclosed shelter, rigged of timber, tarpaulin, and two giant boulders. In a low, tremulous voice, Tegala sang sad songs of unrequited love, a counterpoint to the wind's resounding hymn to winter.

I was up before dawn; perhaps it was the silence that awakened me. I stepped out of my tent and looked upon the immense white pyramid radiant in the moonlight. Jhomo Lhari's glazed, shiny surface, unmarred by crevasses, filled half the sky with its pristine beauty. It was an awesome sight, exhilarating and utterly breathtaking—an extravagance of nature. I slid back into my sleeping bag, anticipating the prospect of another memorable day in a land not as perfect as Shangri-La, but equally intriguing.

E very movement has meaning in the sacred drum dance (left), performed at a religious festival in the village of Talo. Monks act out the triumph of good over evil to ensure the welfare of the community. In a fearsome animal mask, a layman at the Paro festival (above) plays the part of a raksha, *a participant in the judgment of the dead.*

FOLLOWING PAGES: *Intent audience gazes at dancers at the Tongsa Dzong. Bhutanese dance-dramas teach the lore and values of Himalayan Buddhism.*

ayside shrine, a
chorten *presides over*
cloud-veiled Dochhu
La, a 10,233-foot-high pass
on the serpentine east-west
highway. Such monuments pay
homage to Buddha or to other
religious figures and protect the
area from demons. Fluttering
prayer flags, printed with
sacred verses that rise
heavenward with every breeze,
also fend off danger—and bring
merit to those who place them
here. At left, senior monks in
yellow brocade vests gather with
novices outside the Mongar
Dzong in eastern Bhutan. By
tradition, many families enter
a son into a monastic order.

Simple fare of rice, barley, chilies, and tea makes a midday meal for a family of yak herders at home on the remote northern border with Tibet. Their diet also includes butter, cheese, and dried meat provided by their yaks. In summer, these hardy, seminomadic people drive the shaggy beasts to lofty pastures. Most Bhutanese live by farming and raising chickens, pigs, and cattle in fertile, well-watered valleys.

FOLLOWING PAGES: Below the snowy bulk of Jhomo Lhari, a pony caravan nears a crumbling 17th-century fort that once guarded this frontier against raiders from Tibet. "When I stepped out of my tent and saw Jhomo Lhari, dazzling in the morning sun, it seemed as if great trumpets were sounding," said the author, who camped in a snow-frosted meadow at the base of the sacred mountain.

ASIA

In Bhutan I had entered a world profoundly different—enthralling in its strangeness, its complexities, and its beauty. Such wonders abound in the immensity of Asia, with its harsh deserts, steaming jungles, sacred volcanoes, and stupendous mountains. The largest continent, Asia is home to nearly three billion people, who inhabit timeless villages or thronged, turbulent cities where blue-tiled mosques, marble palaces, or gilded pagodas hint at a glorious history.

I do not recall when I first felt the allure of Asia. Certainly reading the Arabian tales of *The Thousand and One Nights,* Rudyard Kipling's stories about India, and Joseph Conrad's accounts of life in the islands of the eastern seas created a desire to roam those distant lands. In museums I marveled at Persian miniature paintings, Siamese bronze Buddhas, and treasures from the tombs of Mesopotamia.

It was a dream come true when I first traveled to India. Since then I have strolled many labyrinthine alleyways redolent of spices, where merchants sit cross-legged in open-fronted shops; I have entered numerous temples where the tinkle of bells and the scent of incense fill the air; I have ambled along dusty roads, chaotic with rumbling bullock carts and bicycles, and watched farmers toiling in tea gardens, on rubber plantations, and in terraced rice fields. There is endless variety in the pageant of Asia—its parade of women dressed in saris, ao dais, kimonos, or swathed in veils; its assortment of craftsmen weaving silks glittering with gold thread, shaping pottery of perfect proportions, creating colorful images of countless gods.

Asia has long fired the imagination of the West with its opulence and oddities. The Orient beguiled Alexander the Great, who more than 2,000 years ago conquered Persia and reveled in the sumptuous cities of Persepolis and Babylon. Others ventured across Asia in quest of its riches. Merchants in camel caravans and seafarers in wooden dhows brought silks and spices, pearls, gems, and ivory, and fragrant sandalwood and camphor to the patricians of the Roman Empire and Byzantium.

Asia's reputation for luxury persisted through Europe's Dark Ages and in 1260 lured the Venetian traders Nicolo and Maffeo Polo across the sandy wastes of Tartary. Sixteen-year-old Marco joined his father and uncle on their second journey, an incredible overland trek to China, to the opulent court of the Mongol potentate Kublai Khan. In a book that became an instant sensation, Marco Polo firmly established Asia's fame as a realm of the fabulous and fascinating.

The centuries have robbed Asia of some of its extravagances, but the Vale of Kashmir remains as lovely as when the rulers of India's Mogul Empire summered and dallied there, in the Gardens of Shalimar. Masterworks of architecture such as Bangkok's Temple of Dawn still cast their spell. And the rock gardens of Japan provide Buddhist monks with the same perfect places for meditation as they did hundreds of years ago.
                                                                —*Cynthia Russ Ramsay*

Masterpiece in marble, India's Taj Mahal so harmoniously combines dome, cupolas, and minarets that the structure seems to float. Floral inlays adorn the walls of the 17th-century memorial to love, built in Agra by the Mogul emperor Shah Jahan as a tomb for his favorite wife.

DAL LAKE
India

I n the pale light of morning, a water taxi glides across *Dal Lake in the Vale of Kashmir.*
Famed for its gardens and the houseboat-hotels on its placid waters, the mile-high
Himalayan valley has been a resort for centuries, an escape from the heat of India's plain.

arren spires of the Karakorams tower over the long-isolated Hunza Valley. The mountain range contains 60 peaks above 20,000 feet and numerous major glaciers. In this arid land, farmers rely on waterways fed by melting ice to irrigate patches of arable soil.

Fiery glow of the sun silhouettes the Temple of Dawn (left). This landmark, with its five rounded spires, looms over Bangkok's Chao Phraya River. Below, a saffron-robed monk crosses the rear courtyard of the ornate Marble Temple. An image of Buddha stands under the gilt canopy, guarded by two marble lions. Havens of calm and centers of learning, more than 300 temples uphold Buddhist traditions in Thailand's crowded, cosmopolitan capital.

85

F ading light of day touches the roof of the world, the Himalayas. Mount Everest, whose summit appears at left, crests the range at 29,028 feet, on the Nepal-Tibet border. The Sherpas of Nepal honor earth's loftiest peak as "Goddess Mother of the World."

KYOTO
Japan

Trained in etiquette and the arts of music, dance, and conversation, a geisha (opposite) embodies the elegance and beauty of old Japan. She acquired her skills in a special school in Kyoto, cultural and spiritual capital of Japan for more than a thousand years. In springtime, cherry blossoms grace the Shinto Heian shrine (above), built in 1895. Raked gravel and rocks evoke a landscape of flowing water and mountains for a Zen Buddhist meditating in the garden of Kyoto's temple Daisen-In (left).

HUANG SHAN MOUNTAINS
China

Mystical as a Chinese
painting, the summits
of Huang Shan float
above encircling clouds (right).
Ancient pines grow from rock crevices
among the jagged peaks (below).
These mountains rise from a single
granite massif in Anhui Province,
southwest of Shanghai. Hot springs,
waterfalls, and crystalline pools
enhance this popular retreat.

prawling Potala Palace commands the heights above Lhasa, Tibet. Legend says the palace holds more than 1,000 rooms, 10,000 altars, and 200,000 statues. Now a museum, the citadel once was home to the Dalai Lama, Tibet's exiled ruler and spiritual leader.

WILD REALMS

DAPPLED SKIES OUTLINE AN ACACIA TREE ON TANZANIA'S SERENGETI PLAIN.

EAST AFRICA

By Chris Eckstrom Lee
Photographs by Medford Taylor

Africa unbridled came to camp the first night with a song of the plains primeval. Through the silence that brings the heartbeat to the ears, I heard the faraway rhythm of drums, like a sound that drifts into a dream. More drums joined in, the pace quickened, and the drumming rolled toward camp, louder and more insistent, with the rumble of an approaching longhorn stampede. Dust swirled around the tents as a great herd of zebras galloped past in wild flight, their strange, high whinnies and thundering hoofbeats slowly fading as they vanished in distance and darkness. In the stillness that followed, a lion growled a deep, aching groan, giving voice to the uneasy hours of darkness that concentrate the senses to a point like the tip of a spear.

There is beauty and fear in the sounds of the African night, and they excite imaginings as powerful as the mythic daytime visions of a continent whose very name suggests the primitive, the prehistoric, the unknown. The night sounds are the murmurings of Africa, ancient and wild, and the calls seem to reach across space and time to a place within us that remembers them.

The zebras gave me a heraldic bush greeting in the savanna of northern Tanzania as I began a safari through East Africa's Great Rift Valley region, a land of lemon-gold grasslands streaming with antelopes, huge soda lakes flushed pink with flamingos, lone mountains wrapped in snowy capes that rise above equatorial forests, and apocalyptic desert moonscapes that challenge the barest notion of life. It was a safari through a landscape of high drama, and a journey to understand the place that Africa's wild beauty holds in the minds of those who have known her land.

So mysterious was the interior of Africa that until the mid-19th century the continent could still be described as it was in the Bible: "the land shadowing with wings." Africa's highest mountains and biggest lakes, the headwaters of the Nile and the Great Rift Valley, remained unknown to the outside world.

It was just before the turn of the century when a Scottish scientist named J. W. Gregory ventured into East Africa's wilds and made the first geologic exploration of the Rift, a gash in the earth extending some 4,000 miles from Syria to Mozambique—about one-sixth of the world's circumference. The valley is so gigantic that Gregory believed it would be visible from the moon; pictures taken on the Apollo missions do reveal the Rift to be one of earth's most conspicuous land features.

The Rift marks the boundary where a huge segment of earth's crust has been slowly breaking apart for millions of years—creating what may one day become a new sea. A chain of great lakes lines the valley floor, and dozens of volcanoes rise along its length, giving the region some of the continent's most breathtaking scenery. Where it slices down the length of Kenya and into northern Tanzania, the Rift is a broad, sunken corridor, in places more than 25 miles wide, its walls sometimes

Fierce will of the predator finds undisguised expression in the eyes of a lion, symbol of the wild spirit of East Africa's Great Rift Valley lands, where an array of national parks and game reserves protect a treasury of African wildlife.

thousands of feet high. Between its escarpments and in the surrounding highlands can be found a showcase of Africa's natural wonders—and a terrain that still looks, to each new eye, like explorer's country.

I was in sacred land the night the zebras fled by, camped by Ol Doinyo Lengai, the "mountain of God" to the Masai who roam the Rift region around the border of Kenya and Tanzania. Rising like a pyramid from the valley floor, Lengai is still active, last erupting in 1966. It stands alone, faintly smoking, a signal of the earth-moving forces that formed the Rift—and proof, to the Masai, that God lives there.

Lengai was a fitting place for photographer Medford Taylor and me to start a journey around and up the valley. In Tanzania, we traveled in old-fashioned, canvas-tent style, guided by Peter Swan, an Australian with 15 years of experience leading safaris in Africa, and accompanied by a crew who set up spacious tents for each of us—and one for dining. At the end of each day the crew welcomed us with cool drinks and a cheery campfire, the mellowing nightly venue for trading thoughts and tales, where we listened to animal cries in the darkness and savored the sweet dry scents of the savanna. Much of Peter's life has been spent in the continent's wilds, and one evening he remarked, "Even after I leave, when I'm home in Australia, I can still smell Africa. I'm sure I always will."

Our comfortable safari was spare compared with the expeditions of the mid-1800s, when explorers such as Burton and Speke set off from Zanzibar and headed inland with hundreds of porters lugging everything from beds, swords, and umbrellas to boat-building tools, a blacksmith shop, and a modest library. Led by a flag-bearer and a drummer, they marched perhaps ten miles a day, with the porters sometimes carrying the weary explorers in hammocks.

Some days, when we made excursions from camp, we also covered about ten miles, but we traveled the modern way, bouncing around Africa in a Land-Rover—a ride that feels a bit like being towed along a rocky riverbed inside a lightly padded crate with a view. Occasionally, a pair of young Masai warriors would appear before us, barefoot, red-robed and unencumbered but for their spears—like visitors from another world and time. They would survey our vehicle and possessions with a look of perfect disdain and then wander off into the empty plain, softly chattering and laughing together, as if we were the very pith of humor. I shared their sentiments whenever the vehicle broke down; then, it seemed that the 20th century itself had failed, and gazing at the Pleistocene world around us, I would have gladly traded all I had for what the Masai know.

A man of the early Pleistocene would feel at home around Lengai, for the land looks much as it did a million years ago. I had camped there several years before, and to me it is a magical place, where you feel the sheer immensity of Africa, a land of such enormous scale that out on the plains a giraffe can look like a distant sapling, or an elephant a stone. From the base of Lengai a sea of long grass rolls away endlessly north; to the south loom the evergreen volcanoes of the Crater Highlands, gloomy with mist. Kilimanjaro hides in a castle of clouds to the east, and beyond the high Rift wall to the west the Serengeti Plain stretches away toward Lake Victoria, the blue-water eye of the continent. The views seem bigger than the sky, the horizons more far-reaching than those at sea. The vastness of the landscape confers at once a buoyant sensation of natural freedom and a great humility, the way you feel when you consider the stars at night, and the uncountable worlds winking above.

Africa is like a love and a heartbreak. Fresh from safari, author Isak Dinesen

Vast canvas of African landscapes, the Great Rift Valley region of Kenya and Tanzania holds a panorama of the continent's natural wonders—from the desert bushlands of Lake Turkana to the rippling Serengeti savannas and snowcapped Mount Kilimanjaro.

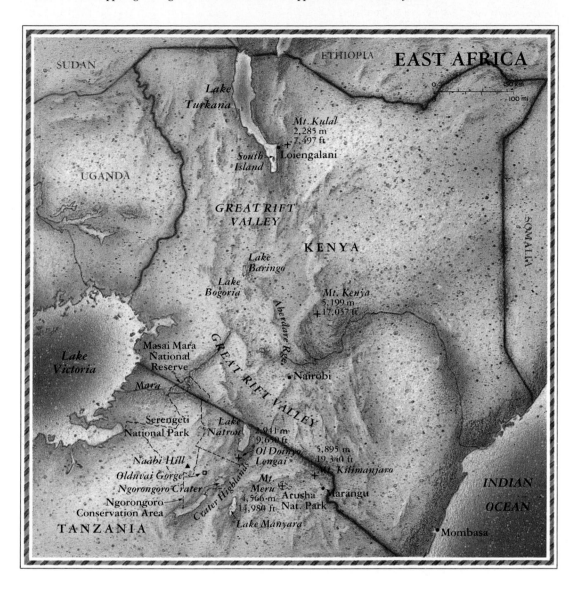

wrote that she had "just emerged from the depths of the great wide open spaces, from the life of prehistoric times, today just as it was a thousand years ago . . . strengthened by the air of the high mountain region, tanned by its sun, filled with its wild, free, magnificent beauty in heat-dazzling days, in great clear moonlit nights." In the *Green Hills of Africa,* Hemingway felt the pain: "All I wanted to do now was get back to Africa. We had not left it, yet, but when I would wake in the night I would lie, listening, homesick for it already."

Sometimes the plains seem to be a landscape of loneliness. Driving around Lengai country, we passed animals alone or in far-apart pairs: Two ostriches kick a dusty trail across the flats; two gerenuk bound off through the scrub in long, elastic leaps; a lone wildebeest stands in tall grass, his beard blowing. The animals look surprised to find themselves there, as if they had just been created—spun from the dust devils that twirl high cones of powdery soil across the valley floor. Then, in the distance, a solitary Masai warrior walks like a first man, silhouetted against Lengai, his robe billowing in the wind. Tall and slender as his spear, he is an image of both a primitive age long gone and the essence of the modern existential man.

The presence of the Masai is felt throughout this Rift Valley region, where they have roamed for centuries. Even where they no longer live, their memory survives in place-names, legends, and in the tales of the tribes they fought. In their time, the great-grandfathers of the various young warriors we saw probably would have savaged us, for the Masai were once the terror of East Africa, and their ferocious reputation kept their lands among the last explored on the continent.

When a young Scot, Joseph Thomson, decided to journey through Masai country in 1883, the great explorer H. M. Stanley reportedly told him, "Take 1,000 men or write your will." Of his first encounter with the Masai, Thomson wrote, "We soon set our eyes upon the dreaded warriors that had been so long the subject of my waking dreams, and I could not but involuntarily exclaim, 'What splendid fellows!'" Within days he was running for his life from the splendid fellows, retreating to Mombasa at a jog. He later found a route through Masai land, returned to a hero's welcome in England—and inspired a new enterprise in Africa, the safari business.

Being on safari is a little like traveling on a local train. You rush past a thousand impressions, your eyes panning the land like a movie camera; then you pause, now and then, at a whistle-stop, to investigate a scene. North of Lengai, we stopped on the flats by Lake Natron to watch one of the Rift Valley's most sublime spectacles: tens upon thousands of bright pink flamingos feeding and flying along the shore. The flats bordering Lake Natron are so bleak and colorless that the sight of the flamingos is almost shocking, like a red dress at a funeral. In a country of creatures that match the grasses and trees, the flamingos are comic relief to the searching eye, a soothing counterpoint to camouflage. The flamingos can dare to be showy in their soda lake home because few other living things will set foot there. From a distance, the lake seems serene and inviting, its waters a mirror of the sky, but Natron can eat your clothes, skin, and bones—and can bring death to animals that drink there, but not to the dainty flamingo.

Like most of the lakes that spangle the Rift Valley trough, Natron is bitter with sodium carbonate, a substance found in the volcanic ash that dusts the land and in alkaline springs feeding the lake. The soda waters bloom with blue-green algae that flamingos thrive on; their bills are adapted for straining food from the water, and they rinse off and drink daily in fresh springs. For the flamingos, Natron is a liquid fortress, where they may blush rosy in defiance of predators, but to naturalist Leslie Brown, the most famous researcher of flamingo behavior, it was "one of the foulest spots on earth," a ghastly place "glittering evilly in the sun."

Leslie Brown learned the horror of the lake firsthand, while attempting to solve "the mystery of the flamingos." Some four million lesser flamingos—two-thirds of the world's total flamingo population—live in Africa's soda lakes, but until the mid-1950s, no one knew where they bred. The Masai said that the fledglings emerged, like spirits, from the waters of Natron. In a feat that rivals the adventures of the early explorers, Brown made a grueling walk through the "vile mudflats" and "pink, stinking water" of Lake Natron to find the birds' secret nesting site, making one of the great ornithological discoveries of the century—and nearly losing his life.

To me, perched on a rock island on the mud flats by the shore, the shallows of Natron looked calm and silvery, like a pool of mercury. I watched the flamingos stroll above their inverted reflections, stepping through pictures of clouds from the sky, thrumming with contentment—pretty creatures, as Leslie Brown wrote, "inhabiting a world only they can inhabit with enjoyment."

The flamingos of Natron are a prelude to the epic-scale pageant of wildlife that lies just over the Rift wall to the west in the Serengeti, home to the most spectacular concentration of large wild animals in the world. Most of these two million or more animals are wildebeests, and they define the limits of the Serengeti-Mara ecosystem—a region larger than Vermont—by their annual migration route, traveling north to Kenya's Masai Mara National Reserve then back south to Tanzania's Serengeti Plain, following the shifting cycle of rains that green the grasslands.

When they graze the Serengeti, the wildebeests present a folk-art portrait of pastoral tranquillity, peppering the plains, as peaceful as cows. Then, suddenly, they go. The wildebeests are the largest herd of migrating animals on earth, and watching them in migration is like seeing an instinct take form before your eyes. I have seen them on the move, from the ground and from the air, dark streams of animals braiding channels through the grass to the far horizon, racing rivers of wildebeests, running head to tail across the savanna as if the land had been tipped and all the animals were pouring down like liquid. They move like a single thing driven, with a will that knows not what force urges it on, the spirit of wilderness taken shape in a torrent of beasts. The Serengeti looks melancholy when the wildebeests have gone; their trails groove the dry hide of the land like old scars, and here and there a horned skull whitens in the sun. I remember clouds of yellow butterflies around the plain, delicate winged things that seemed to be swirling in the wake of the big migration.

The wildebeests had just departed when we arrived, but the rest of the Serengeti's vast panoply of creatures remained, a picture-book treasury of African wildlife: Cape buffalo grazing along a river; giraffes poking up through tall acacias; lions lounging on the plain. The beauty, variety, and wildness of its land and animals have brought fame to the Serengeti, and its protection as a national park has attracted scientists who study the web of life in an intact and unspoiled ecosystem—one of the only places in Africa, or the world, that preserves such an ark of life.

How does a scientist view this land? One morning before dawn, I drove from our camp at Naabi Hill, by the park border, in search of cheetahs with Dr. Tim Caro, a British scientist who studies what is perhaps the most elegant and sensational predator of the African plains. He has followed the cheetahs of the Serengeti since 1980, and he knows most of them by sight and by the names he has given to them.

We headed north to the Gol Kopjes, an archipelago of rock islands that shelter little oases of fig trees, acacias, and wildflowers—and offer a perfect vantage point for big cats to survey the plain, hidden among the rocks. "You find that cheetahs tend to sleep in the most beautiful spots," Tim said, "and that's not just chance—it's probably got a lot to do with safety. We also enjoy places where we feel secure, and our aesthetic judgment may, in part, have something to do with safety. I'm always amazed that when I'm with the cheetahs, we end up in nice places in the evenings."

A new cheetah, a young male, stepped into the sunlight by the island known as Castle Kopje. Sleek and streamlined, he radiated raw, contained power. He seemed too muscular to be merely walking; his body is built for the explosive, paws-out sprint, and I ached to see him run. He turned to glance at us, then slinked up into the kopje to an overlook high in the rocks, nestled among bushes of white blossoms, where he watched a large herd of gazelles grazing below. The cheetah sat stock-still; we waited for his move. Minutes passed. The gazelles edged closer to the kopje, oblivious of danger; the cheetah seemed cagey—he hadn't moved a muscle.

But I think if we could have seen his face, we would have found that his eyes had closed. He settled down in the warm rocks, like a bored house cat, and fell asleep.

Cheetah research involves a lot of time spent attending dozing cats. "Still," Tim said, "if you're interested in animals, the Serengeti is one of the paradises of the world—and it's one of the last strongholds where we can learn about African animals in the wild. To me, the fact that I was born in the right century to see all of this is just incredible. I still get the feeling that I'm privileged to be here."

On the eastern edge of the Serengeti Plain rise the Crater Highlands, a cluster of extinct volcanoes reaching heights of 11,000 feet, their rims dark with forests that catch low clouds and turn them to mist. Deep inside the caldera of the old volcano known as Ngorongoro lies a 100-square-mile microcosm of the Serengeti paradise, a thumbnail sketch in the highlands of the great plain far below.

From the rim of Ngorongoro, you can see the entire crater floor in a sweep of the eye. Near the center, a soda lake gleams in the sun, its waters pale pink with rafts of flamingos. Straw-colored grasslands fan out from the lake, yielding to green river swamps and woodlands near the caldera walls, which surge up like ocean swells to shelter the crater world. Flotillas of clouds sail from rim to rim, their shadows easing imperceptibly across the crater floor, as if they were a visible measure of a slower passage of time. It seems not quite a part of the rest of the earth, a place where the mountains are offering up a small chalice of African land to the heavens above.

We descended into the crater—2,000 feet from rim to floor—along a pitching, zigzagging, rock-and-dirt road. "Part of the track out of the crater follows elephant trails," Peter Swan said, "because elephants are such good judges of the best way to go. Although," he added, "some places are so steep that they slide down on their rumps." There were elephant signs all along the track: tunnels of trampled bush through the forest, heaps of dung in the road, and abstract murals of tusk-mark designs gouged in the crater's walls, where the elephants dig the soil for minerals.

While animals occasionally move in and out of the crater, a Serengeti sampler of wildlife—lions, rhinos, hyenas, and jackals, herds of wildebeest, zebra, buffalo, and gazelle—thrives inside the Ngorongoro bowl year-round. Our camp was set in a grove of trees near Loitokitok Springs, where fat hippos loll away the day, bathing their sensitive hides ("they sunburn," Peter said), emerging after dark to graze. In camp at night, we could hear them grunting, and I wondered, in whatever long-ago era they came, how the hippos climbed down into the crater—and knew that a freshwater home would be there.

Our tents were pitched where the first European visitor to the crater, Austrian explorer Oskar Baumann, camped in 1892. He shot a number of rhinos nearby, and reported on the site with the sportsman's sensibilities of his time: "For a hunter our camp would be paradise. Close to the small wood were numerous guinea-fowl, of which I shot a few for breakfast. Hippopotami snorted in a pool and terrific herds of game were roaming in the wide plains; they were hardly shy at all. . . ."

One morning an old bull elephant passed near camp on his way down to the spring, hardly shy at all, and close enough for us to catch his ripe animal scent. He moved as slowly as the clouds above, his tusks shining white in the dull light of overcast skies. He was the same old bull I had seen once before, walking toward me from the misty walls of the crater, unhurried but full of purpose, like a prophet returned from the wilderness bearing a revelation. He rocked from side to side with each step, trunk swaying, ears flapping, his progress as rhythmic and hypnotizing as the swinging pendulum of a grandfather clock. He reached a bright green swamp and inched down the slope to feed, coiling his trunk around bundles of grass and curling them up to his mouth. Behind him, young gazelles scampered in the yellow savanna, ephemeral lilliputian fawns next to the colossal bulk of the old bull. Yet he was no less graceful, only slower, and I watched him for nearly an hour, transfixed by the simple beauty of an elephant eating grass. Among all the creatures of Africa, only elephants, by their mere presence, seem to elicit such awe. They make you fall silent, stop you in mid-thought, as if a king had just entered the room, unannounced. I suppose that 50 years ago, the old bull would have made a fine trophy for a hunter, but today I am content with him as a keepsake in my mind's eye.

The ancestors of elephants had not yet even evolved into mammoths when the Rift Valley began to subside some 10-to-20 million years ago. The same geological forces that created the valley kindled the volcanic fires that gave birth to the Crater Highlands and thrust up, 100 miles to the east, the towering peaks of Kilimanjaro, the crown of the continent. Although stories of Kilimanjaro had circulated for centuries among Arab traders on the East African coast, it was only in 1848 that a missionary named Johann Rebmann could report the sensational news that he had seen a snowcapped mountain just below the Equator. Scholars laughed, arguing that it was impossible for a snowy peak to exist in the tropics, and more than a decade passed before two Europeans attempting the first known ascent of Kilimanjaro confirmed the truth of the snows.

I first saw the mountain from horseback, riding through rain forest between Kilimanjaro and Mount Meru, a pretty little sister peak to the west. At the crest of a hill, Kilimanjaro made a ghostly appearance. With its base lost in haze, the mountain seemed afloat in the sky, its presence defined only by the snows—like knowing, by his white smile in the dark, that the Cheshire cat is high in the tree. Kilimanjaro is such a compelling beacon in all the countryside it commands that even as we cantered through a woodland jewel box of greenery I found myself peeking through branches to see if the mountain was there. Land-Rover weary, I had set out to experience a tropical forest from horseback, in the fashion of the early colonial settlers. I rode through lands along the border of Arusha National Park with Mafalda von Kalckreuth, a venerable equestrienne who has lived in East Africa so long that she waves off the question with the suggestion that we give the horses a good run.

Across grassy fields, over a rushing stream, and through a meadow of herbs that tingled the nostrils, we climbed the slopes that led into the lofty world of the forest, where suddenly the air was moist and cool, as if, from the noon of a hot summer day, we had entered an old stone cathedral. Up high, tropical boubous called to each other with hollow pipe-and-bell songs as we wound past olive trees shaggy with old-man's beard, and 100-foot-tall junipers, their boughs rustling and bouncing with diving blue monkeys. We rode through aisles of fragrance, of sweet mountain flowers and rich, damp earth, into a settlement of small farms, or shambas, where the smell of wood smoke hung in groves of papayas, bananas, and coffee. People stared and waved shyly as we passed, and I could still hear the barnyard music of cows and roosters, dogs and sheep, as we trotted into the wild woodland again.

Just past the edge of the farms and the forest, we rode by a gnarled old African olive tree. Its branches were silky with colobus monkeys, their tails flowing like feather boas as they leaped among the boughs, their screech-and-grunt cries mingling with the distant laughter of children from the shambas, in a curious babel of wild and domestic Africa. Then, in a clearing on the trail back to the stable, I saw Kilimanjaro's snows turn rose in the sunset—and disappear in a veil of clouds.

An Arab legend describes Kilimanjaro as "an enchanted mountain, which moves about, which one seeks to reach and where one never arrives," and it seemed to be true the day I set out to hike the parklands below the summit. I didn't intend to climb the mountain, but neither, it appeared, did the Land-Rover: Just below Marangu, the jumping-off village for climbers, the vehicle choked to a halt, and while Peter Swan took it to town for repair, I decided to make a different hike, a leisurely ramble up to the park, through the world of the people of Kilimanjaro.

The white skies had tumbled down the mountain the morning I set off on my walk, and the air was so cottony with fog that people looked to be wandering in and out of the clouds. The road cuts through the land of the Chagga people, and its vertical course seems to lead through one long, extended village going straight up the mountain and into the sky. The road was a grand promenade, like a combination of county fair, Saturday market, and busy day on Main Street in a rural town—in Africa. I passed groups of old men leaning on canes and chatting in the street, strings of cattle, their humps wagging, boys seated beside neat pyramids of tomatoes and onions for sale, children chewing sugarcane, and women gliding smoothly along with gigantic loads balanced on their heads—bunches of bananas, bundles of maize stalks, baskets, firewood, sacks of salt.

Around homes and shops along the road I saw shoe repairmen and wood-workers, men bent over sewing machines making jackets, women planting seeds, people slaughtering sheep, and a girl braiding cornrows in her young friend's hair. Burlap sacks spread with drying millet patched the road, and a machine chugged in a shed grinding the millet for the home brew called *mbege*. A few times I was beckoned toward the pungent smell of fermentation to sample a bit of toddy.

Radios played African chants; church bells tolled iron echoes down the valley; and as I walked I listened to the lilting, musical speech of a people who must be in love with the sound of words—and who never failed to greet me with the Swahili *"Jambo!"*—surely the heartiest hello of any language in the world.

In their tongue the Chagga use the name of Kibo, the highest peak of Kilimanjaro, in expressions of beauty and blessing, and in their fables mountains become people, conversing and acting with instructive humor and humanity. When I spoke with Zuberi Mchawala of the Marangu Teachers College, he told me, "For the Chagga, Kilimanjaro is life itself, like the Nile to the Egyptians. It is where they have lived for all time, and all their beliefs are tied to the mountain." So strong is their identity with Kilimanjaro that Chagga folklore says, of the origin of the people, that they were born of the mountain.

The clouds had furled back up to the snows by the time I headed down, lifting a curtain on the great stage of plains and distant hills below, vistas that must be painted in the minds of the children of Kilimanjaro. Three young men asked me if I had succeeded in climbing the mountain, and I said that I had only hiked along the road, but that I had seen what I wanted to see, even from right where we stood.

Africa's beauty has a faraway quality that can change to a cruelty on close inspection: The lovely, lenticular acacias of the plains will snag and prick; dramatic expanses of stones cut the feet; the waters of sparkling lakes are undrinkable; and there are fangs and claws in the forest that I hope I never encounter. Such is the beauty of the frontier district of northern Kenya, where Medford Taylor and I flew at the end of our safari to visit the elemental land of Lake Turkana, the famed Jade Sea in the heart of the desert.

From Nairobi, we soared north in view of the jagged peaks of Mount Kenya, over the hills of the Aberdares, where waterfalls plummet in long, silver strands through bamboo forests, past the blue-gem lakes of Bogoria and Baringo to the badlands that rack the land south of Turkana. Mazes of buttes dropped down to a hard plain so veined with waterless rivers that it resembled a sky full of lightning forks. In places, the rocks looked barely cool from the violence that had formed them, and the whole scene seemed pre-man or post-man, but not of our time on earth. When Count Samuel Teleki explored here and named the lake Rudolf in 1888, his companion, Ludwig von Höhnel, described the land as a veritable hell. Finally the lake appeared, twinkling and green, as startling as a flowering tree in a winter forest.

We stayed at the doum palm oasis of Loiyangalani, between Turkana and Mount Kulal, which funnels winds of up to 80 miles per hour across the oasis and the lake. Out from Loiyangalani, desert bushland stretches seemingly to infinity, quivering in heat that makes wide, watery mirages in the sky. Along Turkana's shores Richard Leakey and a team of paleontologists have found fossils they identify as the remains of early men dating back more than 1.5 million years. So eroded is the land that Leakey spotted one find, a skull, literally staring up at him from the earth.

The inheritors of the land of early men roam the lake country: Turkana, Gabbra, Samburu, Boran. Near the lake I watched Turkana tribesmen herd goats to shore for a drink, in flocks so huge and massed that from afar they looked like a white-capped bay. The land is so parched that the animals seem to eat the earth, and it is hard to imagine what sustains them. What we ate, every day, at every meal, was fish, fresh from the Jade Sea. In an earlier era, Turkana was connected to the Nile, and as a reminder of that time the lake teems with zeppelin fleets of Nile perch, a delicious fish that can tip the scales at nearly 300 pounds.

On a day when the wind was sweet and the sky bonnet-blue, Medford and I decided to go fishing in the desert. Grand Canyon colors tinted Mount Kulal as we trolled the waters around South Island, one of three volcanic isles in Lake Turkana, where giant fish bones litter the beach and the dreaded Nile crocodile lurks in the shallows. We dreamed of a big Nile perch that would make us proud, and worried that it might capsize the 20-foot boat. Then Medford's rod tip dipped, and we shouted with joy as he reeled in. The fish didn't resist, and as it neared the boat, we could see that it was a bit small; in fact, it weighed four pounds. Medford, who enjoys fishing, told me a lot about his luck when he said, "Biggest fish I've ever caught."

That night the wind howled from Mount Kulal, tossing the palms of Loiyangalani, making them roar like the ocean. I stood outside in the gusts, feeling the hot, dry breath of Africa and staring up at the arc of diamond constellations in the black new moon sky, stars that guide the navigators of the desert just as they do those at sea. Dry thunder boomed from Mount Kulal: The Gabbra believe it is the drumbeats in the sky of a young girl seated on a lion skin who was carried off in a whirlwind; she beats the skin when she is frightened, and the heavens rumble. At this tiny oasis by the lake, I was swept up in the sounds and visions and fears of the continent where man was born, with the sensations of a land known to the early men whose bones bleach in the desert nearby. Under the glittering bell of the night sky in a world that seemed just made, I felt as I had in all of Africa's wild space, a witness to the beauty of creation's inspiration.   ᴸ🔺ᴶ

FOLLOWING PAGES: *Sunlight rains through a caldron of clouds to the floor of Tanzania's Ngorongoro Crater. Forested walls 2,000 feet high enclose the 100-square-mile caldera, an extinct volcano that shelters woodlands, swamps, and savannas teeming with wildlife.*

Herders of the savanna, Masai nomads tend their cattle in the Ngorongoro Conservation Area, a reserve that includes Olduvai Gorge—where paleontologists have found fossils they identify as remains of early men who roamed the area some two million years ago.

nimals sociable and solitary find a niche in Kenya's Masai Mara National Reserve: A leopard claims a camouflaged perch, and hippos keep cool in the Mara River. To the south, in Tanzania's Lake Manyara National Park, a baboon grooms a fellow troop member. Masai Mara marks the northern reach of the Serengeti-Mara ecosystem—home to the most spectacular population of big wild animals in the world.

PRECEDING PAGES: Shoals of wildebeests massing for their annual migration stream across the plains of Tanzania's Serengeti National Park.

Huddled impala does warily survey the grasslands of the Masai Mara National Reserve. The rolling plains, savanna woodlands, and riverine forests of the reserve support 20 species of antelopes—and nearly 100 of Africa's estimated 1,500 species of mammals.

Serene spectacle of flamingos feeding along the shore of Lake Natron belies the harsh nature of these soda waters—caustic and undrinkable to most creatures, but rich with blooms of algae that nourish flamingos and redden their plumage (right). The Great Rift Valley gleams with a chain of soda lakes that provide sanctuary, food, and nesting grounds to millions of flamingos.

RICHARD PACKWOOD/OXFORD SCIENTIFIC FILMS (FOLLOWING PAGES)

*FOLLOWING PAGES: Everlasting
snows of Kilimanjaro whiten
the furrowed slopes of the
19,340-foot-high peak, the
tallest mountain in Africa and
crown of the Rift Valley region.*

117

AFRICA

Remembering Africa, I see the great white eye of the full moon giving pale form to the landscapes and animals I have watched in the night, and I think of the eyes of the continent that have looked into mine—the gaze of four giraffes standing side by side; the red eyes of hyenas just beyond the campfire; the tracking stare of gazelles as I passed them on the plains; and one charming time, at a camp near Lake Natron, the lively, unfearing eyes of a Masai girl who came with her father to shake my hand and say hello. I have spent my time in Africa in the wild country that still dominates the continent, and that shapes both the character of the people who live there and the imaginations of those who dream of what Africa holds.

"There are many Africas," wrote author Beryl Markham. "Africa is mystic; it is wild; it is a sweltering inferno. . . . It yields nothing, offering much to men of all races." Africa has always inspired great quests. Explorers in the mid-1800s ventured into interior lands that remained as uncharted a century ago as they were when Ptolemy made his map of the world around A.D. 150 and identified most of Africa as terra incognita. Their expeditions unveiled Africa's natural wonders, places with a power to awe undiminished since the time they were first seen by the eyes of the outside world: Victoria Falls, the Mountains of the Moon, the peaks of Mount Kenya and Kilimanjaro; the Rift Valley region lakes of Victoria, Tanganyika, and Malawi; and the heart-of-darkness rivers of the Congo, the Niger, the Zambezi, and the Nile. Africa is the keeper of the treasures of ancient Egypt and the kingdoms of Ghana, Mali, and Zimbabwe. It carries the sand seas of the Sahara and Namib, and expanses of forests and plains that shelter some of the greatest populations of large wild animals on earth. The continent so long mysterious to the outside world holds the bones of our earliest known ancestors, the brittle clues to the origin of man.

I remember the moon's slow descent in the sky when I flew across the Mediterranean and down the continent to Kenya, and I remember that every time I looked, I saw only a few scattered stars of light from the earth until the twinkling constellation of Nairobi appeared. When the sun rises, it brightens a continent where cities seem like atolls in an ocean of wild land. Of the vastness of the continent, South African author Laurens van der Post wrote, "One goes on for thousands of miles. One goes on until one's eyes and limbs ache with the sight and bulk of it."

Africa's wild nature is the wellspring of its beauty, and the reason that people will continue to search for what Africa never yields but always offers. I have a memory of that feeling from a bumpy, four-wheel-drive descent through the bamboo forest of Mount Kenya. A leopard, a creature now rare and always rarely seen, stepped into the track before me, and for a long moment, I met his green-eyed stare. An instant later, he melted into the bamboo, leaving me with a look into the eye of unknowable wildness that is the essence of Africa.   —*Chris Eckstrom Lee*

Desert idyll of palms and pastel buildings, the oasis village of Tafraout nestles against the granite hills of Morocco's Atlas Mountains. Nomads of the Sahara come to Tafraout to trade, and visitors journey to discover a picturesque but little-known corner of Africa.

*P*erfect peaks of the Pyramids of Gîza rise from the Sahara on the west bank of the Nile, where earth's greatest desert meets its longest river. The ancient Greeks regarded the monuments— old even in their day—with awe, proclaiming them one of the world's Seven Wonders.

VICTORIA FALLS
Zimbabwe-Zambia

"*S cenes so lovely must have been gazed upon by angels in their flight,*" *missionary-explorer David Livingstone wrote of Victoria Falls in 1855. Here, waters of the Zambezi plummet 355 feet, creating what Africans call the "smoke that thunders."*

125

Elephant cows and their young gather to drink from a water hole in Namibia's Etosha National Park. The preserve—larger than New Jersey—contains a Noah's ark of more than 80,000 African mammals, part of the continent's incomparable wildlife heritage.

FOLLOWING PAGES: Shifting dunes of the Namib Desert capture Africa's changing drama.

SOUTH AMERICAN

WONDERLANDS

SMOLDERING CONE OF CHILE'S VILLARRICA LOOMS IN SIGHT OF DISTANT LANÍN VOLCANO ON THE ARGENTINE BORDER.

LAKE REGION

By Tom Melham
Photographs by Nicholas DeVore III

Call it love at first sight—though wine played a supporting role. Back in 1977, Juan and Alexandra Braun attended a party in south-central Chile, some 500 miles away from their Santiago home. The town was Lago Ranco, which sits beside a rather remote lake of the same name and is accessible by a twisted, thoroughly potholed dirt road. The Brauns drove the entire 500 miles—and immediately were captivated by the jumble of hills and mountains that stair-stepped irregularly up from the lake's southeastern end. Sugarloaf humps rose near the shore, backed by multiple tiers of sculpted cliffs and gouged ridges, while beyond loomed the snowcapped cordillera of the Andes.

Fueled by such stunning natural beauty and several aperitifs, Juan recalls, "We got started talking about how great it would be to live here. Of course our friend giving the party said, 'Yes, yes, yes. Everyone who comes here says that—and forgets the next day.'" But not the Brauns. The next day, with their host as guide, they looked up several local landowners and convinced one to sell them a lot over-looking the lake. Lacking the necessary cash to seal the deal, says Juan, "I took my Austin into the nearest town and sold it for the down payment. That night, we went back to Santiago by train." Impulsive? Of course. But the Brauns followed through on their decision to move—despite nagging doubts over cutting themselves off from friends and the urban familiarities of Santiago. For one thing, Juan's job in international pharmaceuticals had become increasingly burdensome. "I was spending more time in a plane each week than I was spending with my family," he says. "That's when I knew I had to get out."

Now, Juan keeps mostly to the ground, rambling across a neighbor's pasture in search of edible mushrooms, perhaps, or inspecting lush beds of dahlias that adorn the Braun home. Lago Ranco's rich soil and ample rainfall, coupled with the Pacific Ocean's ameliorating effects on temperature, make it a garden spot. Juan's *hortensias*—hydrangeas—routinely reach six or seven feet in height and produce flowery heads a foot in diameter. Some he raises for sale, while Alexandra designs wool rugs and organizes local women to weave them. The road to Lago Ranco today remains as potholed as ever—and the area's scenery is as enchanting as the day the Brauns bade farewell to their Austin.

The lake the Brauns fell in love with is only one of several dozen adorning *la región de los lagos*—the lake region—a water-dappled chunk of southern South America that stretches some 200 miles from Chile's Pacific coast across the Andes into Argentina's fabled Patagonia. North to south, this region spans more than 300 miles. Its features range from the exclusive lakeside resorts of Villarrica and Pucón—favored by Europe's contemporary royal families—to the rural island of Chiloé and the stark, expansive vistas of Argentina's Chubut Province. Volcanoes stud the region, often

Wearing a grin as warm as his poncho, Lorenzo Pillipillán totes his purchase home from market on the shores of Lake Villarrica, in Chile. Rustic settings of the Andean lake region combine with posh resorts and national parks in an international travel mecca.

towering up from the edge of a silvery lake, their massive cones seeming to float on the water, shimmering mirage-like in the morning mists.

While most of the area's glacially spawned lakes hug the spine of the Andes, the lake region enfolds a far broader realm, one that includes lively port cities such as Valdivia and Puerto Montt as well as numerous national parks, thermal springs, and ski areas. The region's core of snowy peaks and sparkling lakes creates a strong alpine feel, at times bolstered by chalet architecture that reflects an influx of Germans and Swiss a century ago.

Throughout, the land offers an impressive, often contradictory, variety of forms: volcanoes and glaciers, dense forests and open rangelands, rocky seacoasts and hills patchworked into farms and woodlots. Similarly, travelers may find themselves sampling a hotel's international cuisine one day—and sharing a peasant's roasted armadillo the next. Organized tours, including a bus-and-boat crossing of the Andes, coexist with less regimented forays into trout fishing, boating, horseback riding, and alpine sports. Map distances can be deceiving in this land where roads are few and often unpaved. But each area claims its special charms, both physical and cultural.

There is, for example, the Jamaica-size island of Chiloé, which hugs a notch in the mainland just south of Puerto Montt. Chiloé is something of a microcosm of the lake region, offering all sorts of environments, from coastal marine and *tepual*—a local wooded marsh—to lake, forest, and mountain habitats, including the windblown, tundra-like *turba*. This island's rich life-forms—especially its birds and marine mammals—attract contemporary naturalists just as they drew the attention of Charles Darwin when his ship, H.M.S. *Beagle,* put in for a two-week stay here in 1835. In between hunts for hummingbirds and eight-foot-wide leaves of local *pangue* plants, Darwin one night witnessed from Chiloé the "magnificent spectacle" of Osorno, a mainland volcano some 80 miles away, in full eruption.

Today, in addition to views of gleaming volcanoes, Chiloé boasts a 106,000-acre national park. Its Cordillera de Piuchué provides an island counterpoint to the majestic Andes. The surrounding ocean makes snow a rare event here, despite latitudes comparable to those of Montana. Poised before the predominant westerlies, Chiloé offers weather so changeable that an islander warned, "You can experience our four 'seasons'—cloudy, sunny, rainy, windy—all in a few hours."

Although the Spanish began to settle on Chiloé as early as the 16th century, the island continues to maintain a certain isolation and appeal. Even today it harks back to another time, another life-style. Some of the island's 116,000 residents still rely more on horses and oxcarts than on cars and trucks, and their primary occupations tend toward the traditional: farming, fishing, handicrafts. Those reared in Chiloé's more remote areas continue to speak an archaic Spanish, in some ways closer to the language of the conquistadores than to that of present-day Santiagans.

Architecturally, Chilotan towns seem a mix of Wild West and New England: The buildings, invariably of wood and often unpainted, frequently stand packed together like a row of weathered frontier facades. Mostly they are sheathed in handmade shingles that recall Maine or Massachusetts—except that the shingles almost never follow straight lines. Chilotes prefer fancier touches, and so finish each row's bottom edge with a repeating pattern—notches, curves, or slants—that personalizes each house.

Wood is *the* raw material of Chiloé. It provides not only housing but also

transportation (oxcarts, sledges, yokes), local industry (flour mills, cider presses,

134

Glacial lakes of south-central Chile and Argentina jewel the Andean cordillera like a double
string of pearls. This region encompasses craggy seacoast and fertile farmland, lush forest and
open range. A Germanic flavor in many towns reflects waves of 19th-century immigration.

looms, farm tools), and the cheerfully painted fishing fleets that brighten each town.
No fiberglass or superconductors here; even super*markets* are rare, far outnumbered
by open-air *ferias*—marketplaces. Firmly wedded to its past, Chiloé presents visitors
with an alluring time warp. One Santiago woman I met was so won over she proclaimed, "Chiloé? It is *magic.*"

To many islanders, the magic is literal. Chiloé has been a wellspring of
witchcraft and mythology for centuries. Here, the black arts survived not only the
Conquest but also repeated attacks from the local courts. Even today some islanders
say a coven of *brujos*—male witches—still convenes in a secret cave, guarded by a
hairy and horribly deformed beast known as Invunche.

Renato Cárdenas, a native Chilote, developed an early interest in his island's
enduring fascination with the arcane and eventually wrote a book about its traditional beliefs. He told me that quite apart from the brujos, Chiloé claims a pantheon of
mythic creatures, each equipped with supernatural powers. Ravishingly beautiful

135

La Pincoya, a sea goddess, watches over marine life and loves to dance on the water off secluded beaches. Short but strong El Trauco—part satyr, part woodland dwarf—lives in the forest and sires children born out of wedlock.

Apparently, magic and myths are simply part of life on Chiloé. The 1960 earthquake that severely disrupted local shellfish beds serves as an example. Most Chilotan fishermen, says Cárdenas, attributed their poor shellfish harvests then not to the quake but to La Pincoya—who they felt was punishing them for replacing traditional wooden implements with modern, metal clam rakes.

Basketmakers Juan Marilicán and Angela Lindsay, I found, hew to another tradition. They weave uncommonly delicate creations from *quilineja,* a thin woody vine they say is increasingly hard to find. Some might credit the plant's disappearance to a shrinking of the island's forests, but Juan and Angela blame El Trauco, who they believe jealously guards this fiber for his own use—he makes his clothes of it. "When people look for quilineja," Juan told me, "El Trauco makes them lose their way. Sometimes he even makes them go mad. You have to take the vines when he's not looking." Juan was not joking. Had he or Angela ever spotted the dwarf during one of their quilineja hunts?

"No," Juan admitted. "But I've heard his footsteps many times, snapping branches on the forest floor." Angela piped up, "And I've heard the shouts of Invunche. Two short screams, like a goat." I left their house realizing that to them creatures such as El Trauco remain every bit as real as the rooster in their front yard. When I related this experience to Cárdenas, he nodded enthusiastically.

"The people believe La Pincoya and all the other mythological creatures *are* real. They're not religious objects; they aren't worshiped or given offerings or prayed to. They're just part of our natural world."

Chiloé is a bountiful land, rich both in fruits of the sea and those of the earth. Enter any of the ferias that mark a major town and you pass aromatic stalls overflowing with local foods: fresh *robalo* (a white-fleshed fish); rocky heaps of *picorocos* (giant barnacles); dried seaweed, compressed into bricks or tied in ropy hanks (a base for soups and stews); chunks of *congrio frito* (fried conger eel); *machas* and *almejas* and half a dozen other types of clams. Smoked mussels and oysters hang suspended on long string loops like black pearls. Vegetable sellers hawk Chilotan produce: potatoes, oversize carrots, and the island's gargantuan garlic bulbs, which are prized throughout Chile for their sweetness.

"You'll never starve to death on Chiloé," Nicolás Piwonka assured me in the marketplace of Ancud, a port at the northern end of the island. "You always have the sea. And the fields." I learned that Nicolás, a photographer specializing in natural history, had moved to Chiloé from Santiago only five months before. Like the Brauns, he'd decided to trade city life for the allure of the lake region.

"In Santiago now the air is really bad. The people are too nervous and tense. It wasn't like that a couple of years ago. Here, you live in a healthier environment. And even though you don't earn as much money, you don't waste as much, either."

A tradition of bartering helps keep down Chiloé's cost of living, he explained, and islanders often tackle barn-raisings and other big projects by setting up a *minga*—a common work group. Nicolás enjoys such traditions and the sense of community they project. He also savors Chiloé's isolation. "You're on an island, cut off from everything, surrounded by water. I like that very much. It orders my mind in some way."

He adds that while the islanders do work hard, he feels they are not workaholics. Many days, only a few boats venture to sea. The stay-at-homes might say the off-weather heralds a poor catch, or that the market's demand is down, or that they simply have other things to do. The reason isn't important; the attitude is—for it embodies the independent life-style that attracted Nicolás to the island.

A similar yearning for the good life—that is, a more balanced and enjoyable existence, not just a life with more money—brought Adrián Dufflocq and his bride, Patricia, to Llifén, just east of Lake Ranco, in 1963. Today you'll likely find Adrián standing up to his hips in a cold stream, hour after hour. For *fun*. He wears the trappings of membership in a select club: chest waders, poplin vest with lamb's wool patch, and polarizing sunglasses. A $1,500 piece of bamboo extends his right arm and rhythmically wafts back and forth, while his left hand gradually pulls line off a reel and feeds it to the bamboo.

Welcome to fly-fishing, among the least efficient and most satisfying ways for man to land a trout. Nonanglers see its rules as perversely favoring failure. Why else forgo the conveniences of live bait and lead weights, or even employ barbless hooks? Lacking sinkers, the fly-fisherman must rely on skill alone, using the line's modest weight to gain distance in the cast.

Hence the coachwhip motion, seemingly effortless yet terribly precise. Each overhead sweep ends in a barely perceptible pause that allows just enough time for the ever-increasing load of line to follow—but not so much that its momentum succumbs to gravity. Then the final flick of the rod, "shooting" the accumulated line to the target: a widening ripple caused by a passing fin. And then the slow, erratic take-up as the fisherman plays the line, trying to get the inanimate bit of fluff at its end to mimic the lurchings of an emerging mayfly or a drowning grasshopper.

Again and again Adrián repeats this graceful ritual, seeking Zen-like perfection in the ultimate cast. Later, he would show me one of his finely handcrafted bamboo fly rods, proclaim it "a work of art," and shrug off its high cost with the comment, "If you want to drink some nice wine, you want it in a crystal glass, not a plastic cup. This is alive to me; a graphite rod isn't."

The Dufflocqs operate one of Chile's best-known fishing lodges, sought out by the world's top anglers. They picked this area, says Adrián, for its "tremendous watershed—five or six rivers of different shapes and habitats." Each stream possesses a fairly gradual gradient, sparkling clear water, good gravel beds, and a rich source of food—the basic requirements for trout, which are in abundance here and can sometimes weigh as much as 20 pounds. Best of all, they are *wild* trout.

Introduced to southern Chile in the early 20th century, rainbow and brown trout were not periodically restocked. To Dufflocq, this means the fish have had decades to develop traits shared by wild animals: wariness and the will to survive. "There's always the temptation to introduce more trout into these rivers every year. And that can be the biggest mistake," he cautions, for farm-raised trout lack the stream-wise characteristics of their wild cousins. In other words, even *I* might be able to land one of them.

Dufflocq's surname is French, just as photographer Nicolás Piwonka's stems from Czech origins, and Juan Braun's reflects German ancestry. All three men were born in Chile. Though their names may not sound Latin American, neither does the name of the nation's 19th-century liberator: Bernardo O'Higgins, an illegitimate son of one of Chile's last royal governors, Ambrosio O'Higgins. Chile, like the United States, traces much of its heritage to Europe. The lake region is linked especially to Germany.

The first Germans came here in the 1850s, when the Republic of Chile—then just over 30 years old—began enticing European farmers with offers of land. The government's motivation stemmed largely from its desire to gain real control over the part of the nation that in some ways still belonged to Mapuche Indians: the area south of the Bío-Bío River and north of Chiloé, which includes much of the lake region. Not even the mighty Inca had succeeded in conquering the people there. Nor had Spain, although it had claimed sovereignty over what it called the Araucano—Mapuche—lands for some 300 years.

And now the fledgling republic, seeking a way to succeed where two military empires had failed, decided to rely less on soldiers and more on settlers. It was a tactic often used in North America, and it would work here equally well. Europe's farmers, largely unaware of any Indian hostilities in Chile, were suffering various disruptions brought about by the mid-19th century—economic depression, famine, political upheaval, and various growing pains of the Industrial Revolution. Many were only too ready to cross the Atlantic.

One who did was Friedrich Grob, who left Dresden for the lush, rolling country midway between Valdivia and Osorno—which reminded him of southern Germany. Grob started a flour mill in the town of La Unión in 1865, and helped found the local German club and German school. Today, his great-grandson Teófilo Grob runs the family's much-expanded milling operations; he also belongs to the club, which still boasts the best restaurant in town. Weekends and holidays, Teófilo usually unwinds on his private, 400-acre island in the middle of Lake Ranco, amid woods stocked with deer originally imported from the Hamburg Zoo.

"A good place to relax," he allows modestly as he takes in sensational views of glaciated valleys and Andean peaks, "and to preserve nature."

Like many of La Unión's older residents, he speaks German as fluently as Spanish. Up until 25 or 30 years ago, plays and shows held at the club were performed in German. But now La Unión's German-ness has begun to fade.

German club president Ricardo Preisler scoffs good-naturedly at the increased usage of *Laguna Deutsch*—literally, "lake German"—an informal blend of German and Spanish comparable to the "Spanglish" often encountered in Miami or New York. He regrets such changes but feels powerless to prevent them from continuing. "After four generations," he says, "the people here don't feel German. They *aren't* German." They're Chilean. Even those who go abroad to study usually return home to work, according to Preisler.

And yet an unmistakable German presence still colors much of the lake region. Some houses in the town of Frutillar alongside Lake Llanquihue sport the window boxes, square shutters, and balconies of the classic chalet. Streets bear names such as "Carlos Richter" and "S. Junginger," while a local cafe offers German *Kuchen* (cake) along with Spanish *pan* (bread). Signs advertise not only a roadside *hostería* (inn) but also a *Gasthaus* (guest house) and *Bierstube* (bar). All of this bolsters the town's overall impression: Bavaria with an Andean backdrop.

Germanic styles and traditions also flavor the area's larger cities, notably Osorno and Valdivia in Chile, and the Argentine resort of San Carlos de Bariloche, a metropolis of some 80,000 on the shores of Lake Nahuel Huapí. Popularly abbreviated as just "Bariloche," this city freely combines aspects of chalet architecture with unadorned Bauhaus design; it also features Swiss restaurants, chocolate factories, and a serious preoccupation with alpine sports. Ski lifts trace nearby Cerro Catedral, one of several craggy peaks that early European immigrants compared to the Alps. Bariloche's population has always been international; for that matter, so has Argentina's.

Alumine Yerio, who runs one of Bariloche's many tourism operations, considers her country "the most European in South America. In its outlook. In everything." Born as a colony of Spain, Argentina welcomed immigrants from so many other nations, says Alumine, that "Today there is not yet such a thing as an Argentine name. We are Italian, Scottish, German, French, Swiss, Arab, Jew, Greek. We are all *puros por cruza*—pure mix. It will take another century or two for us to develop an Argentine stock."

One of the area's early settlers was neither German nor Spanish, but a Texan named Jarred Jones. He and John Crockett—one of Davy's descendants—arrived in 1885 with hopes of perpetuating the cowboy life they loved but could no longer pursue in North America's dwindling Wild West. They worked Argentine cattle for a while before Jones started a ranch bordering the northeastern section of Lake Nahuel Huapí. Jones also built a general store, which became a favorite way station for English-speaking travelers. Western hospitality was always on tap, and a large round table that could seat eight in comfort was just perfect for poker.

In the autumn of 1901, the story goes, three Americans—two men and a woman—arrived in Argentina. The Americans had been granted some land in tiny Cholila, a settlement in Chubut Province to the south of Nahuel Huapí. They occasionally stopped by the Jones ranch, the men passing time in numerous card games. The leader, about 40 years old, was an affable sort, accomplished at poker. He went by the name of James Ryan, though he had been christened Robert LeRoy Parker. The world knew him by yet another name: Butch Cassidy, the Mormon-turned-highwayman whose infamous Wild Bunch ravaged the western U.S. up to the turn of the century. The gang's string of successful holdups eventually resulted in the hiring of Pinkerton detectives. Cassidy soon departed for South America, where he traveled in the company of a "Mr. and Mrs. Place," none other than Harry Longbaugh—the Sundance Kid—and his lovely girlfriend, Etta.

Contrary to Hollywood's version of their life stories, the trio left New York not for Bolivia but for Argentina—partly for the same reason that Jarred Jones had gone there: to live in the open spaces of this sprawling cattle country. In time they set up a ranch in Cholila, where they lived for about five years. Even today people still recall their stay here. Constancia Freeman de Owen, born in 1897 in Chubut's Welsh community of Trevelín, remembers their visits when she was a girl:

"They were good gauchos—horsemen, you know, well trained and very, very active. When they came along, we used to admire their American saddles and all. They had very good horses. Place and Mrs. Place were very tidy people from the city, you could see that. But Ryan was more of a regular cowboy, a *ruffian*. He had coats with fringe and all that type of thing. They used to stay at our house. They'd say they needed to give the horses a spell, then they'd go on. We never knew they were bandits until years after."

For the most part the three lived quietly—an easy thing to do in remote, sparsely populated Cholila. Etta, however, seems to have been somewhat flamboyant. According to locals, she established herself as a fine horsewoman and was said to be a better shot than either of her companions. No one seems to have suspected the *norteamericanos* of foul play, despite reported sightings of their sizable arsenal and of stolen cattle on their ranch.

In time, the three returned to their prior vocation, enlisted some former members of the Wild Bunch, and pulled off a number of heists. And then—well,

Connie Freeman says they just rode out of her life. Today, some residents claim that "Ryan" and "Place" assumed new aliases but were caught and executed by police in Río Pico, Argentina. Others say the pair died in a blazing shoot-out around 1909, in Bolivia—or somewhere else. The variations are many and contradictory, well muddled by time. Butch's sister, Lula Parker Betenson, wrote in her 1975 biography that her brother stopped by her Utah home for a slice of homemade pie in 1925, more than a decade after his supposed demise!

Whatever happened, the gang's T-shaped cabin in Cholila still stands, its squared logs overlapping at the corners and chinked with mud. One wing remained tantalizingly locked when I visited in 1987, and neither the owner nor the current tenant possessed the key. The whole structure had settled a foot or more since Butch's day, and the floorboards had rotted into dirt—but here and there a few scraps of ancient floral wallpaper recalled happier times. Just back of the cabin, a silvery stream continued to burble on, while distant peaks capped a lonely and wild land strongly reminiscent of the Utah badlands that Butch loved.

"I like the place better every day," Butch wrote a friend in 1902. "I have never seen finer grass country, and lots of it hundreds and hundreds of miles that is unsettled and comparatively unknown. . . ." His words more aptly describe lands northeast of his ranch: Argentina's fertile pampas, home today to some of the world's best beef. Cholila country appears somewhat drier and leaner—more crag and tussock than endless sea of grass, possessing an overriding feel of emptiness that makes its small, scattered towns seem yet smaller and more isolated.

E ven cosmopolitan Bariloche, on Patagonia's northwestern fringe, is dwarfed by the land's vast open spaces, overwhelmed by its gorgeous alpine and subalpine scenery. Within sight of this city, snow-clad Mount Tronador—The Thunderer—crowns the Andes divide with rumbling avalanches and icefalls that eventually feed glacier-carved lakes in Chile as well as in Argentina.

The region's numerous natural charms moved naturalist-explorer Francisco "Perito" Moreno to cede a tract of land back to his nation in 1903, on condition that it be preserved forever in its natural state. Formally organized in 1934, Nahuel Huapí National Park continues to honor that stipulation while it also adds immeasurably to the local economy.

Nahuel Huapí ranks as one of Argentina's largest and most popular national preserves, claiming upward of 500,000 visitors yearly. Moreover, it provides about 160 full-time jobs—more than a fourth of all national park positions throughout the country, and enough to make it one of the area's major employers. The park's name—taken from spidery, seven-armed Lake Nahuel Huapí—stems from a centuries-old Indian phrase that translates to "island of the tiger."

No tigers roam the park, but indigenous pumas do, as do llama-like *guanacos* and rare, spaniel-size *pudúes*—the world's smallest deer. Park environments vary from scrubland to thick forest, with most visitors seeking out an alluring middle ground of blue, transparent glacial lakes rimmed by forested shores and mountain views. To North Americans, the local trees can appear to be from some exotic, alien realm: The thin, waxy leaves and cinnamon-colored bark of the *arrayán*—a local myrtle—seem more attuned to a Walt Disney animation than to reality. Dense stands of full-boughed *coihué* and *lenga* lend a wild feel of the totally primeval. Tall, cone-bearing *alerces* resemble California's redwoods—but only to a point, appearing familiar yet different.

North of Bariloche, the land itself grows quirky. A stretch of steepening riverbank known as Valle Encantado—Enchanted Valley—erupts with increasingly bizarre rock jags. Breccias born of old lavas rise up atop dry hills, burnished by the autumn sun, while rustling Lombardy poplars shed their yellow leaves in a golden snowfall. Farther along the valley, gnomic sentinels of rock give way to crenulated and deeply pocked promontories that seem more overgrown fungus than stone. Other formations recall Utah's Bryce Canyon, but in subtler shades: mauves, greens, and grays. The valley's name fits: Its stony projections are so sharply sculpted that their nicknames—"cockscomb," "mermaid," "finger of God"—demand no imagination from the spectator; the rock possesses more than enough on its own.

To the east the land is less broken, a rolling realm of tussocks and occasional mesas. Here the rock weathers more secretively, spawning few spires but numerous caves. The area is called Pilcaniyeu—from a Mapuche word—and many of its caves still retain reminders of a pre-Mapuche people. I explored a few of these caves with Adam Hayduk, an archaeologist from Bariloche. Bits of chipped stone, broken animal bones, and occasional fragments of human remains litter the floors, while dynamic and colorful pictographs flow across the walls. Some of the caves have not yet been fully studied by archaeologists, and even today we are still learning about the early artists who created these works.

We do know, Adam explained, that they engraved most of their pictographs into the soft, light-colored stone; over time, smoke from campfires blackened the etched lines. More recent designs were painted in natural pigments of yellow, red, or white. Often the subjects of the pictographs were animals, displayed realistically but minimally: Usually only a creature's footprints appear, not its entire body. The effect is powerful and somewhat eerie, as if the animal had actually entered the cave and boldly scrawled its signature on the wall.

At one site, a puma's black paws ghost silently across the cream-colored rock. At another, deeply etched shapes mimic the tracks of a *choique,* or rhea, which resembles the African ostrich. A third wall bears cloven hoofprints of the guanaco. And then, suddenly, rock paintings of total abstraction: here a repeating stairstep pattern, there a labyrinthine "maze"—which some archaeologists feel may symbolize the road departed souls must travel on their way from earth to heaven. But, Adam observes, no one really knows.

While Adam and I looked about, a pinch of brown duff in one cave immediately drew his attention. "Fantastic—this grass means the cave is unusually dry. It still may contain basketry, weaving, wood and other organic materials of the society that lived here—not just stone tools. Such finds are not common." An instant later, his delight collapsed into disappointment. "But you see these recent holes in the floor? Someone digging for supposed gold or silver treasure. It's a pity."

Happily for the viewer but unhappily for the art, these caves are open to all. You need only step inside; some of the paintings before you have survived more than a thousand years, despite the ravages of erosion and of man. I especially recall a stylized human figure, sparely yet elegantly portrayed in a few curving lines of red ocher. It stood alone at one cave entrance, catching the morning light as it gazed out upon a sprawl of river, tussocks, and mesas.

Was this figure a guardian spirit? A talisman to ensure success in some long-ago hunt? A celebration of human triumph, perhaps? Or was it merely Stone Age graffiti, as indecipherable when new as it is today? No matter—its presence lends an enduring magic to these walls, and that magic adds to the special enchantment that is *la región de los lagos.*

*N*ear-perfect symmetry of Chile's lordly Osorno Volcano lends a Fuji-like grace to its snow-clad bulk. Visible from 50 miles away, Osorno reigns within Vicente Pérez Rosales National Park, oldest of the country's 30 national parks. The Argentine portion of the lake region offers equal spectacle. A wrought iron patron saint (below) watches over Lake Moreno, foreground, and Lake Nahuel Huapí, central attraction of Nahuel Huapí National Park. Scoured by glaciers and hemmed in by peaks, this long, narrow, multiarmed lake reminds many of Switzerland's Lake Lucerne.

Outdoorsman's paradise, the lake region draws boaters, hikers, skiers, and fishermen. Guide Adrián Dufflocq (left) casts a line below Chile's Nilahue Falls, near Llifén. The region embraces a wealth of pristine waters ideal for trout, introduced here at the turn of the century. A jug of wine, a loaf of bread—and a freshly caught brown trout— fulfill an angler's vision of perfection (right). Stony outcrops along Argentina's Traful River (above) evoke the unfettered feel of the American West.

Tradition travels well in Angelmó, Chile, a wharfside section of regional capital Puerto Montt. Horse carts still haul the day's catch to local markets and restaurants. The port's handicrafts center features weaving and basketry from nearby Chiloé and other islands.

E choes of Europe resound through the lake region, where German and Swiss farmers settled more than a century ago. Above, Angela Barría of rural Chiloé Island proudly displays a portrait of her mother, a German immigrant. Near the Argentine town of Llao Llao, the log Chapel of San Eduardo (right) seems almost Alpine in style, though it owes its design to 20th-century Argentine architect Alejandro Bustillo.

FOLLOWING PAGES: Bewitching as any desert mirage, an Andean amalgam of fog, lakes, and mountain ridges shimmers in ever changing light.

SOUTH AMERICA

From first glimpse to final farewell, my journey through South America's Andean lake region revealed a land at once familiar and exotic. To me, its mountains and arid stretches recall parts of the western U.S. Its lakes evoke those in Europe's Alps. Its fishing villages resemble Portugal's. It is the *juxtaposition* of these very different features that makes the region so exotic, so alluring.

So it is with the entire continent. Physically, South America is a realm of extravagances. Its Andes constitute the world's longest mountain range, higher than any save the Himalayas. Its Atacama desert is the world's driest. Its massive Amazon dwarfs all other rivers. And its vast rain forest ranks as earth's largest.

Like the U.S., South America is a cultural melting pot. It is also our nearest continental neighbor. Yet strangely, it remains a place little known by many U.S. travelers. Every year, we visit Europe in far greater numbers than we venture south of Panama. We do so partly for business, partly because we are creatures of habit, partly because the human animal tends to overlook nearby attractions.

Nearly 500 years have passed since Columbus anchored off what is now Venezuela, on his third voyage of discovery. Spain and Portugal soon divided the New World's southern half, conquered and colonized it, and managed for several centuries to seal it off from the rest of the world. And so South America remained shrouded in mystery into the late 18th and even 19th centuries, when naturalists and other men of science began to penetrate the continent's great unknowns—men such as Charles Marie de la Condamine, who descended the Amazon and returned to France with samples of rubber, curare, quinine, and other New World wonders. Alexander von Humboldt probed remote reaches of the Orinoco River and Rio Negro, scaled peaks in Ecuador and Colombia, and gathered enough information on plant life, geology, climate, and geography to publish a 30-volume treatise.

Then came Charles Darwin, eagerly cataloging the wildlife of the Andes and of the Galápagos Islands as he proceeded on his lifelong journey of discovery and revelation. A similar sense of exploration and discovery carried over into the 20th century as well. Not until 1911 did Hiram Bingham set eyes upon the glorious Inca ruins at Machu Picchu—overlooked by countless conquistadores.

Even today, myriad unknowns lurk in the green vastness of Amazonia; the magnificent Andes continue to awe and to dominate; uncloaked and largely unpeopled Patagonia is still a gloriously wild, windswept link between the continent's bulk and frigid Antarctica. Quite apart from such wilderness charms stand South America's storied cities: Rio de Janeiro basks in one of the world's most spectacular natural settings, while Buenos Aires offers a truly cosmopolitan culture spiced with European joie de vivre. In short, South America's manifold enchantments stand alongside the world's best.   —*Tom Melham*

World's highest waterfall, Venezuela's majestic Angel Falls shrinks a passing plane, right, to gnat size. The falls plummets down the face of Auyán-Tepuí mesa for 3,212 feet—including an initial free-fall of just over half a vertical mile—before joining the Churún River.

RIO DE JANEIRO
Brazil

"The marvelous city," Brazilians call Rio de Janeiro, where legendary beaches and forested hills such as Sugar Loaf, at upper left, provide a natural backdrop for a city of 13.5 million. The capital until 1960, Rio remains Brazil's cultural and tourism center, drawing travelers with chic shops, endless nightlife, and attractions that include 100-foot-tall Christ the Redeemer (left), poised atop Corcovado hill.

Maelstrom of cataracts and eternal mists rages endlessly in rock-strewn Iguaçu Falls, on the Brazil-Argentina border. With a national park at each end, the falls—known as Iguazú in Argentina—spans some two miles, about three times Niagara's width.

MACHU PICCHU
Peru

Timeless splendor of Machu Picchu crowns a saddle 8,000 feet up in the Andes, northwest of Cuzco, Peru. The magnificent stonework of the citadel—undiscovered by the outside world until 1911—reveals the genius of 15th-century Inca architects.

TORRES DEL PAINE NP
Chile

Gnarled sentinel, a wind-sculpted tree frames a hiker viewing the tortuous Horns of Paine in Torres del Paine National Park, near Chile's southern extreme. In this remote realm live guanacos (above), condors, rheas, and other wildlife. An iceberg (right) drifts on a glacier-fed lake even in summer.

FOLLOWING PAGES: *Granite fantasia capped in slate, the Horns of Paine bear the marks of centuries of wind and ice.*

161

MOSAIC

DAYBREAK FIRES THE FOGGY COAST OF BRITISH COLUMBIA'S MILBANKE SOUND.

INSIDE PASSAGE

By Thomas O'Neill
Photographs by Tom Bean

I t is summer and the light seems ever reluctant to leave the sky. Great journeys have begun along the edge of the continent, from the Strait of Juan de Fuca on the Washington-British Columbia border to Glacier Bay in Alaska's Panhandle. Salmon by the million are migrating from the North Pacific, fighting their way up rivers to the tributaries and creeks where they were born and where they will now spawn and die. Killer whales, their high black dorsal fins slicing through the water, are congregating in sheltered straits and bays to feed. Brown bears are leaving the mountains and gathering at stream mouths where they will gorge on salmon.

Humans are on the move as well. Residents of the coastal settlements are climbing shadowy trails to bushes teeming with ripe blueberries and salmonberries. Locals and visitors alike have boarded kayaks and canoes, sailboats and speedboats, and are exploring ice-chilled rivers, inlets braided with waterfalls, islands where eagles and ravens glide. Fishermen at the wheels of seine boats are searching deep waters for salmon runs. And from the south, their whistles echoing off rock and tree, come the ferries and cruise ships, on excursions spanning the length of the coast, their courses set on the watery trail known as the Inside Passage.

The axis for all these northern journeys, the Inside Passage goes straight to the heart of some of the most dazzling wilderness in North America—a thousand miles of wild coast, of fjords and rain forests, hot springs and glaciers. By itself, the Inside Passage describes the natural waterway that runs between Seattle, Washington, and Skagway, Alaska, threading its way up channels and sounds protected from the swells of open ocean. On a larger scale, the Inside Passage has come to signify the whole of the spectacular maritime country that lies along the British Columbia coast in Canada and the southeastern fringe of Alaska.

Another name for the waterway is the Marine Highway. Because almost all the coastal towns—faces to the water, backs to the mountains—are inaccessible by road, the waterway serves as a lifeline. Where Indian war and trading canoes, sailing ships laden with sea otter pelts, and steamers overflowing with gold stampeders once plied, today freighters and ferries make their way.

Ferries are the workhorses of coastal travel. British Columbia ferries daily crisscross the southern tier of the Inside Passage, linking Vancouver Island, the Queen Charlotte Islands, and the Canadian mainland. The Alaskan state ferry system encompasses all 1,142 miles of the Marine Highway—the longest ferry route in the world. Its main-line vessels, holding up to 980 passengers and 180 vehicles, leave from Seattle or Prince Rupert, British Columbia, and steam for the broken coast of Southeast Alaska. The large, blue-hulled ships pay visits to seven widely scattered Alaskan towns, including Juneau, the state capital; smaller vessels service more remote communities. "Just because it's not asphalt doesn't mean the

Face-to-face with a monumental past, a visitor admires weathered mortuary poles at the abandoned Haida village of Ninstints in the Queen Charlotte Islands. The Haida and other tribes have dwelt along this coast for 10,000 years, sustained by the bounty of forest and sea.

Inside Passage isn't a major road," a Southeasterner made perfectly clear to me.

　　To travel the Passage by boat is to enter an elemental world of rock, trees, and water. Off port, off starboard, mountainsides smothered in evergreens slide by, the forest often so close you can make out the white hoods of bald eagles sitting in the tops of trees. Above the forests, or off in the distance, or down a fjord—rarely out of sight—rise formidable mountain peaks doused in year-round snow. Ahead, the water is often dashed with islands. When the naturalist John Muir traveled the Inside Passage aboard a steamer in 1879, he marveled that "so numerous are the islands . . . they seem to have been sown." What is most striking of all, though, is the immediacy of the wilderness: mountains rearing out of the sea; trees, thick as feathers, growing right to the waterline; all of it closing around you like the walls of a hidden kingdom.

　　During my own journey through the Inside Passage, I hopped off the ferries as often as possible just so I could draw aside the coastal veil and learn face-to-face the secrets of this brazen wilderness. Thus inclined, photographer Tom Bean and I chartered a sailboat in early July and detoured up Jervis Inlet, one of the many magnificent fjords that punctuate the coast. A popular yachting spot for Canadian and U.S. sailors, the long, winding fjord slices into the British Columbia coast just north of the city of Vancouver. Clear skies dyed the water a brilliant blue as we sailed up the inlet in light winds. Steep forested walls escorted us.

　　We were lucky with the weather. The Inside Passage coast is regularly washed by moist ocean air that rides in on southeasterly winds. Clouds sift through the trees like wood smoke; the sky hangs low like a covering tarp for weeks at a time. In such conditions temperate rain forests of spruce and hemlock grow extravagantly. As a trade-off for long spells of gloomy weather, the coast experiences relatively mild temperatures, the climate moderated by the warm Japan Current offshore. Thus Alaskans jokingly refer to the Southeast coast as their banana belt.

　　As we traveled up Jervis Inlet, however, we weren't thinking about the good weather as much as we were considering the Ice Age. Snow and ice at different times engulfed the landscape. Most recently, during the continent-wide Wisconsin glaciation that began more than 30,000 years ago, ice sheets and snowfields buried most of the Inside Passage coast. The ice piled more than 5,000 feet deep in places, enough to swallow mountains. The slowly moving glaciers acted like juggernauts, crushing and grinding the land features beneath them. When the ice began retreating about 15,000 years ago, meltwater caused the ocean to rise and fill the glacial troughs, creating the fjords of today.

　　Sailing deeper into the inlet, we saw the unmistakable signature left behind by flowing ice. Granite outcrops, the muscle beneath the evergreen cloak, wore long scars where glacier-borne rocks had scraped past. Distinct U-shaped valleys opened high on the mountain walls, their curvature left behind by hanging glaciers. Mountaintops were rounded off like skullcaps. Our boat floated on water charted at 350 fathoms, or more than 2,000 feet deep, filling an underwater canyon ground out by the ice wedge. When Tom and I dove like kamikaze pilots into frigid 50°F water one hot afternoon, so clear and bottomless did the water seem that I felt as though I were swimming above a liquid sky.

　　The most impressive swimmers in all the Inside Passage are the killer whales. Largest of the dolphins and recognizable by their bold black-and-white markings and commanding dorsal fins, killer whales, or orcas, gather each summer in pods, their family groups, to prey on schooling salmon off the Washington and British Columbia coasts. All told, more than 300 of these swift, wide-ranging hunters travel these coastal waters.

To see a pod of orcas prowl along the surface, their rank of dark dorsal fins cutting through the water, remains a matter of thrilling luck. But on the leeward side of Vancouver Island, at its northern end, exists perhaps the most certain place in all the world to see, to study—to marvel at—killer whales. It is a narrow, 40-mile-long bottleneck of water called Johnstone Strait. From July to October the northern community of killer whales—estimated in 1987 at 171 individuals in 16 pods—gathers here to feed and socialize.

Even then orcas refuse to be predictable attractions. Take my first day out on the 60-foot whale-watching vessel *Gikumi,* operating out of Telegraph Cove: We were skunked. Second day in a row for skipper Jim Borrowman. "I'm humbled by nature," he muttered. His network of "spies"—fishing crews, Coast Guard patrols, scientific researchers, and shore residents—had radioed in sightings, but we never caught up with the fast-moving whales. Johnstone Strait at this point seemed oceanic. The next day: "This is Eagle's Nest. A pod is coming your way." A call from a field party of marine biology students with Canada's Department of Fisheries and Oceans sent the 12 of us on board scrambling for vantage points.

Wisps of spray low on the water alerted us to the whales' presence. The spray rose with the moist breath of the orcas, expelled as the warm-blooded animals came up for air. The whales were hugging the shore inside the Robson Bight Ecological Reserve, a 3,000-acre stretch of water designated as a killer whale sanctuary, off-limits to boats when whales are present.

The whales, a group of five, soon left the refuge and steered for the middle of the strait, astonishing us as they surfaced 50 feet from the *Gikumi,* close enough for us to hear the whoosh of air from their blowholes and to discern nicks and scars on their great fins. The largest animal looked to be 20 feet long, with a triangular dorsal fin five feet tall. Though killer whales will hunt seals, sea

lions, the giant baleen whales, and other dolphins, no confirmed report exists of their attacking a human in the water.

Jim lowered a hydrophone into the strait; a speaker on deck immediately began amplifying a series of rapid clicks. It was the sound of the whales, their means of communication. After satisfying their curiosity about the large object that was our boat, the killer whales moved on, porpoising their bodies in and out of the water in graceful arcs, leaving us behind to feel small and utterly terrestrial.

As I moved up the coast, I found that my favorite reading material was the navigational charts. With their contours, depth readings, and water routes, the charts provided clues to the region's geologic history; with the charts' place-names, the human history began to unfold. Ketchikan—"eagle wing river"—and Kitkatla—"village by the sea"—echoed the indelible Indian heritage. Tribes inhabiting the coast for some 10,000 years include the Tlingit, Haida, Tsimshian, Kwakiutl, and Salish.

Jervis Inlet, the Strait of Georgia, and Prince of Wales Island number among the hundreds of names bestowed on coastal features by Capt. George Vancouver. The indefatigable British navigator surveyed the length of the coast from 1792 to 1794 during his unsuccessful search for the Northwest Passage. Islands christened Texada, Cortes, and Sonora hark back to Spanish exploration. Perhaps the most intriguing names of all came from the nearest of the imperial powers. Baranof Island, Zimovia Strait, Politofski Lake, Mount Dranishnikof: They all call up the deep involvement of Russia in the North American fur trade. Russian ships frequented the northwest coast during the 19th century, up to the fateful year of 1867, when Russia sold its vast Alaskan holdings to the United States.

A Russian expedition led in 1741 by Vitus Bering is credited with the first foreign sighting of the Inside Passage coast. In 1804 the Russians planted a rude stockade on Baranof Island and named it New Archangel. By 1860 New Archangel had evolved into the largest port on the Pacific coast and had become the capital of Russian America, with 45 Alaskan outposts. The near-extinction of the sea otter finally compelled Russia to unload its North American colony. Renamed Sitka (a Tlingit name) by the Americans, the former New Archangel, now a scenic lumber and fishing town on the Alaskan ferry route, even today conjures up its distinctive heritage. On the waterfront rises the onion dome of the still-active St. Michael's Russian Orthodox Cathedral, its services conducted in Russian, English, and Tlingit.

The early explorers were often met offshore by Indians who came to trade otter pelts and fresh fish for the white man's iron tools and firearms. The large Indian fleets made an impressive sight—the graceful wooden canoes, sometimes by the dozen, leaping the whitecaps with their high, pointed bows. In the lofty rain forest of Canada's Queen Charlotte Islands, just below the Alaska-B.C. border, I witnessed the ghostly beginnings of one such canoe.

Colin Richardson, a young Haida Indian, led me from Windy Bay into the dim interior of Lyell Island, through one of the last old-growth forests left on this intensively logged coast. Ironically, the oldest of the spruce and red cedar that we passed appeared unearthly, so huge (and rare) are they. Some of the trunks had to be 15 feet in diameter—twice the wingspan of a bald eagle—and their crowns were lost in the canopy, at least ten stories above us.

Colin's whistle pierced the hushed forest vault. I found him kneeling over a fallen, moss-shrouded cedar. "Look!" His hand moved over what was clearly the contour of a boat prow emerging from the ancient log. "One of our people must have started a canoe here," Colin explained. "But something made him quit." The carver abandoned his project at least a century ago, for adult cedars were growing straight and tall from the decaying log.

On the Queen Charlotte Islands, signs proliferate, ancient and modern, of the Haida civilization. Regarded by anthropologists as the most advanced of the Northwest Coast Indian tribes, artistically and in respect to their prowess on the sea, the Haida revered the red cedar. It grows to colossal size on this rain-soaked chain of islands 60 miles off the mainland. From the bark the Haida wove their waterproof clothes. From the massive rot-resistant trunks they fashioned their canoes and totem poles, and the roof beams for their spacious longhouses. The Haida venerated the sea as well; its easily extracted bounty allowed them the leisure to develop a rich material culture and a highly organized system of kinship, ritual, and myth. *Haida Gwaii*— "islands of the people": thus the Haida know their land.

I spent five days traveling with Colin in the South Moresby Wilderness, a 75-mile-long archipelago covering about 15 percent of the Queen Charlottes. Colin works for the Haida Gwaii Watchman, a unique program in North America in that the Haida, the aboriginal population, offer guided expeditions through their home-land. And Colin knew his native grounds well: where to jig for halibut and cast for salmon; how to find the way back through a pathless forest at dark; when to cross wind-chopped waters; where to find a hot spring on a grubby wet day.

During our trip Colin took me to several abandoned villages. North of Lyell Island, we visited Tanu, of which his father is a hereditary chief. Like most Haida villages, Tanu sat above a sloping crescent beach where canoes could be hauled safely above the tide and from which the sea could be scouted for intruders and storms. What remains of Tanu is haunting: A path led past a series of prominent depressions, the site of two dozen longhouses; giant, moss-covered roof beams lay side by side in the pits where they had fallen. Only the cry of a raven broke the leafy stillness.

Collectors long ago removed many of the beautiful carved totem poles that stood in front and at the sides of the houses, poles that with their stylized, fiercely expressive visages of natural and supernatural creatures proclaimed the lineage of the house owner. Members of the two main Haida clans, Raven and Eagle, lived at Tanu. It was abandoned after 1885, following outbreaks of smallpox and other diseases, which killed some 90 percent of the Haida. Today, about 2,000 Haida live in the Queen Charlottes, concentrated in the villages of Skidegate and Masset. Some 6,000 people in all inhabit the island chain.

At Tanu, Colin pointed out fragments of poles, most of them obscured by moss and weathering: here the patterned wing and large oval eye of Eagle; farther on, the barbed teeth and long body of Killer Whale. I asked Colin why the Haida don't save the poles. "The elders deliberated a long time about this," Colin said. "Finally they decided. 'Let the forest take them back,' they said. 'We'll build new ones.'"

Carvers are indeed creating new poles. An artistic renaissance has invigorated the Haida nation. A political awakening has occurred as well. In 1983, the Haida's land claim to the Queen Charlottes was accepted for negotiation by Canada. More recently, the Haida stood up for their most valuable possession—the island wilderness. Supported by environmentalists from across Canada and around the world, the Haida blockade of a logging road on Lyell Island in late 1985 sparked the British Columbia government into suspending clear-cut logging in the South Moresby Wilderness. All logging was officially stopped in July 1987 when the federal and provincial governments signed a memorandum calling for a national park reserve.

"Our people need South Moresby spiritually to stay a nation," Colin said. "We couldn't be a nation in a sea of stumps."

Besides the cultural lessons it offered, Colin's tour gave me a chance to appreciate firsthand the riches of Inside Passage waters and the web of life they support. In our agile speedboat we spotted seabirds—kittiwakes, cormorants, pigeon guillemonts—massed on the surface as they fed on needlefish. Harbor seals lifted gleaming, bewhiskered heads out of kelp patches where they were feeding on schools of fish. On Burnaby Island a midden heaped with discarded clamshells and a gravel beach littered at low tide with abalone, crab, and scallop shells testified to how well the Haida must have eaten at their summer grounds at Burnaby Narrows.

While camping at the same meadowy spot, we took the boat out into the open sea to a solitary, wave-lashed rock, and there pried off two armloads of mussels for dinner. We added to our stores later that night. As a luminous fog bank spread over woods and water, we hooked a coho salmon out in the narrows. The fish leapt three times, its body shining like a silver lure on the bright night. Overhead sounded the beating of an eagle's wings. This salmon, however, was ours to keep.

I reached Alaskan waters aboard the state ferry *Matanuska*. Before the three-tiered, 408-foot vessel had even left its pier in Seattle, the top rear deck had sprouted a bright patch of backpackers' tents. It was as if the tent dwellers couldn't wait for the open air and potent wilderness that lay ahead of them. The slow steady trip up the Passage was scheduled to take 3½ days. Cloistered on board were exactly 494 passengers, cameras and binoculars at the ready. Stiff winds and fits of rain kept most of us inside; the hardier among us circled the decks for exercise or stood braced at the railings, staring intently over the iron-gray waters and into the thickly matted woods.

Inside the staterooms, the tents, the observation lounge, the human compass was pointed north. Excitement seeded the air. Alaska, I quickly sensed, holds on to its image as the promised land. In addition to avid sightseers, Alaskans returning home from "down below," and backpackers eager to begin hiking or paddling into the wilds, there was on board a company of passengers headed north to change their fortunes—or at least make some money.

A trio of college-age women from the Seattle area said they were jumping off at Ketchikan to work at a salmon cannery for the summer. Each hoped to make $7,000 in two months. A quiet fellow in a faded plaid shirt, a large duffel at his feet, said he was on his way from Coos Bay, Oregon, to a logging camp on Prince of Wales Island. "I'll make $14,000 in three months working as a choker, three times what I can back home." For one passenger from Boston, a plumber by trade, Alaska represented a consuming dream. "It's been calling me a long time—you know, the call of the wild," he said, his eyes hidden behind a pair of scratched aviator glasses. "It will be tough, I know, to find a job up in Anchorage. But I'm willing to sacrifice so I can be part of this wilderness."

The *Matanuska* crossed into Alaska shortly after dawn on our second day out. The fanfare began a few hours later when we approached the docks of Ketchikan, our first stop. Bald eagles glided from the treetops; two floatplanes, their engines roaring at open throttle, lifted off from the water amid plumes of spray; a stately cruise ship, the *Cunard Princess,* slipped into its berth; and from a marina several tall-masted fishing boats hauled north, gulls screaming overhead. Welcome to Alaska.

I left the ferry at Wrangell, the next town up the Passage. There was a homespun Fourth of July celebration to entice me, with its logrolling contest, boat races, and a fireworks display over the harbor. More to the point, I was dying to step back into the wilderness. Wrangell itself is a robust settlement of 3,100 people, chiefly dependent on the forest industry. Alaska's largest sawmill sits south of town. The timber, most of which is shipped to Japan, comes from the Tongass National Forest, which blankets 80 percent of Southeast Alaska, and at 17 million acres is the largest national forest in the United States.

In looks, Wrangell is cut from standard Inside Passage cloth. Penned between sea and mountain, the town spreads along the shoreline like tidal drift. A weathered main street runs past rows of false-fronted wooden buildings, reminders of the town's frontier origins. Boats of all sizes are tied up along the wharfs. Totem poles rise proudly from a park. To live in Wrangell, or in any small Inside Passage town, requires loyalty—to the place itself, remote as it is, and to the wilderness looming at its edges. "You have to look at this place and say, 'This is my home.' Otherwise you won't fit in. You have to dig in," insisted Barbara Maenhout, an expatriate from Minnesota who stepped off the ferry 20 years ago and stayed. "What clinched Wrangell for me," said John Vowell, the local hospital administrator who came from Colorado, "was that during my job interview, I looked out the window and saw two killer whales playing in the water outside. It was impressive." "I'm not a 'boomer,'" declared Patricia Ockert, director of the town museum and a California native. "That's a person who came up here for the oil and big money and is now leaving. The rest of us came up for the country, and we're staying!"

The country. In Wrangell that usually means the Stikine River. Long a corridor into the interior for Indians and prospectors, the Stikine barrels down a canyon chute for 330 miles from headwaters in Canada to its delta just north of Wrangell. Friendships are easily made in Wrangell, and less than a day after quitting the ferry, I was riding up the river in an outboard. Richard Kaer, a crab buyer and third-generation Alaskan, was piloting. Leaving the Marine Highway, we gunned up a slough turgid with meltwater from the snow-frosted mountains above us. A northwest wind had shoved away the fog and rain, and sunshine glazed the nubbly tartan green of the forest. Whirlpools snarled the current, marking our path through a web of treacherous gravel bars. We passed waterfalls exploding off granite ledges. Ducks beat silently downriver.

About 15 miles up the Stikine in a narrow inlet, a cold spear of air jabbed my skin. Richard tilted the boat around a bend and facing us in all its white immensity was a glacier. Flowing imperceptibly from a high snowfield, Shakes Glacier spilled from a valley to the water's edge. Carefully we cruised toward its cracked, slowly melting face to marvel at the towers of ice that rose above us. Seeing that the glacier wasn't calving, Richard steered us closer. I stretched and touched the centuries-old ice. It was my initiation into the country.

Not long afterward a floatplane landed me in the rain on Seymour Canal, near the mouth of Pack Creek. I grabbed my pack and splashed ashore on Admiralty Island, some 125 miles northwest of Wrangell. The Tlingit name for Admiralty is Kootznahoo: "fortress of the bears." One expert has estimated there is a brown bear for every square mile here, which would make the island one of the world's most densely populated brown bear habitats. (Alaskan usage refers to a brown bear as a grizzly when it lives in the mainland interior; those that inhabit island and coastal regions are called browns.) Wary and wet, I hiked to a gravel spit overlooking the tidal flat. Yes, there were arresting creatures out here. Two men were sitting in lawn chairs in the middle of a downpour, calmly taking notes.

Robert Fagen, a biologist from the University of Alaska, and Njoroge Muigwa, a graduate student from Kenya, introduced themselves. Along with Bob's wife, Johanna, the men were conducting field studies on bear behavior during that most social of times—salmon feeding season. Bob Fagen, encased in a rubberized rain suit, pointed out a brown bear stalking the tidal flat several hundred yards away. Its powerful humped shoulders were starkly visible under the wet fur. In front of us the creek boiled with the thrashing bodies of spawning salmon. "These bears are wild and dangerous, and we treat them with respect," Bob said, his words as measured as the rain dripping slowly from his beard. "But Pack Creek isn't like any other place. Here we are standing next to a salmon stream. I know there's a mother bear and her cubs in the woods there. This is something you *never* do in Alaska. And you'll notice we don't have a rifle. That's unusual, too. But because of frequent visitors and a hunting ban, the bears tolerate human presence."

The human most associated with Pack Creek is Stan Price, a piece of living Alaskan folklore. Eighty-eight years old, he dates his homestead on remote Pack Creek back to the 1940s and since that time has lived peacefully in the midst of wild bears, even raising a few orphaned cubs himself. I found Stan in his cabin in front of a torrid wood-burning stove. Small and white-haired, Stan showed me the movie camera he uses to film the bears, many of which he knows on sight and has given names. The day before, some bears had wandered into his shed and drunk the 24 gallons of water he had put aside for laundry. "But that's a small price to pay to live with these animals," he quickly noted. Bears are an emotional subject with Stan. He believes they have been unjustly hunted and feared in parts of Alaska, and that they only seem dangerous because of their curiosity. "I'm trying to show that bears are assets," he said heatedly. "They're not here so we can put their skins on floors. A bear gets as much pleasure out of life as we do."

Back outside, a sow and two cubs had ambled from the forest to the creek bed, less than a hundred yards from the viewing spit. Suddenly the mother charged into the creek; amid much splashing she pinned down a salmon with a pie-size paw and then carried the fish in her mouth back to the tiny cubs. Another bear made a mock charge at a browsing Sitka black-tailed deer, chasing it away. The U.S. Forest Service, which administers the Pack Creek site, located in Admiralty Island National Monument, is worried that some bears are becoming too familiar with humans and might attack careless observers. In 1987 nearly 700 people visited Pack Creek, one of several reliable places on Admiralty to view the awesome brown bear. To protect the bears from their own curiosity and to maintain the relative purity of the habitat, Forest Service officials are considering adding restrictions to visitation at Pack Creek.

On this soggy July afternoon at least, the brown bears were absorbed in catching salmon. I counted ten bears. No, eleven. Out on the gravel bar at the mouth of the creek I saw a bear bounding through the shallow water, its long legs flying, water spraying. It could have been fishing, but to me this animal seemed to be seized by the simple wild joy of being a bear.

My journey through the Inside Passage came to a close at latitude 59 degrees, in the iceberg-strewn waters of Glacier Bay National Park. To reach those upper bounds I passed north through the Alaskan ferry towns. In Petersburg the purse seining fleet was returning from a 15-hour opening in the closely regulated salmon season. Pinks and chums by the boatload were being hosed, hoisted, or swept into waterfront canneries. In Juneau, the state capital, four cruise ships were paying a call. In the last 20 years, the industries of government and tourism have outstripped fishing and logging as revenue leaders in the Panhandle. Some two dozen cruise ships made more than 300 voyages up the Inside Passage in 1987, offering a more velvety (and expensive) traveling style than does the democratic ferry.

In Skagway, the final ferry stop and one with highway links to the Yukon and the Alaskan interior, a construction crew was restoring the old Mascot Saloon. The Mascot was one of 80 drinking establishments that served the town in 1898, the year more than 20,000 fortune seekers provisioned themselves in Skagway before rushing to the Klondike goldfields. With the establishment in 1980 of the Klondike Gold Rush National Historical Park, a number of Skagway's evocative turn-of-the-century buildings have been restored, providing visitors with a glimpse of what an Alaskan frontier town looked like—minus the mud, the prostitutes, the gunfights, the runaway horses, the. . . . Each town, even now, is a mere dike thrown up against the wilderness. And always the wilderness is calling, its voice heard in the surge of tide, an eagle's cry, the sharp wind off a mountaintop.

"White thunder" calls from Glacier Bay, where ice calves from glaciers and crashes into the sea. The booming echoed off the mountains surrounding me as a friend and I paddled a sea kayak toward the rugged face of Lamplugh Glacier. One of 16 tidewater glaciers in Glacier Bay National Park, Lamplugh courses from a mountain valley directly into the sea. Glacier Bay itself was filled by one huge ice sheet when Captain Vancouver sailed along this coast in 1794. Since then, with the warming climate, the ice has retreated a full 60 miles, leaving a broad, intricate fjord in its wake. In places, Sitka spruce and western hemlock haven't had time yet to throw their familiar mantle over the ground. Instead, vivid patches of lavender fireweed and low tangles of alder and willow stake out the still raw landscape.

The dimensions of Lamplugh aren't easy to comprehend. Its violently fractured face of blue and white ice stretches for half a mile—three or four city blocks—and stands 150 feet high, the height of a giant red cedar. Its surface rent by crevasses, the ice flow is 16 miles long, issuing from the Brady Icefield, where hundreds of inches of snow a year fuel the creeping glacier. And Lamplugh is growing. While most of the park's glaciers are withdrawing—melting at a faster rate than snow can replenish them—Lamplugh slid forward 200 yards over the previous winter.

Our kayak drifted through a field of icebergs, the recently fallen chunks of ice popping and crackling as they melted. I couldn't take my eyes off the glacier face. The wall of ice spoke of a past primeval and ferocious, one ruled by the elements alone. Suddenly a deep roar started to build; high on the glacier face a large block of ice broke free and with a concussive climax like that of a string of boxcars colliding, it plummeted into the sea. The impact sent waves swelling toward us, and the kayak rose and fell, rose and fell as if we were worshipers bowing thanks.

Glacier Bay is a fitting place to end a migration up the Inside Passage. For in the end is the beginning. The enormous scenery of mountain, forest, and sea that defines the Inside Passage is here in the active stages of creation. The ice grinds and carves; forest seeks a foothold; land buried for millennia begins to emerge. In the stark, dominating wilderness of Glacier Bay, I came to realize that my superlatives seemed intrusive, inadequate. Silence, I ordered myself. Allow the elements to have their forceful say.　　　　　　　　　　　　　　　　　　　　　　　　　　　　　　　　　　　ᴌᴬᴌ

FOLLOWING PAGES: *Evening stillness settles over an inlet near the South Moresby Wilderness, site of a new national park in the Queen Charlottes. A 75-mile-long sweep of islands, the park will preserve some of the last old-growth rain forest on the Inside Passage coast.*

Acrobat from the deep, a killer whale hurls its 8,000 pounds into the air off Vancouver Island. In narrow Johnstone Strait—where the whales pursue migrating salmon—researchers have counted as many as 171 killer whales in summer, perhaps the world's largest congregation.

Approaches to water travel on the Inside Passage vary with the visitors. In Glacier Bay National Park (right), two campers choose the intimacy of a kayak over the luxury of a cruise ship. For tourists and locals alike, however, the most popular water conveyance along the coast remains the ferryboat.

FLIP NICKLIN/NICKLIN AND ASSOCIATES (UPPER)

*S*hed by a glacier, a natural sculpture of centuries-old ice drifts in Tarr Inlet in Glacier Bay. Within the park, 16 glaciers descend from mountains directly into the sea. Besides viewing the thunderous spectacle of calving glaciers, park visitors may catch unforgettable glimpses of wildlife—from puffins to harbor seals to brown or black bears.

FOLLOWING PAGES: *Mainstay of Inside Passage travel, a floatplane passes over merging glaciers flowing from the Juneau Icefield, in the mountains north of Alaska's capital. Such stark visions in stone and ice lend counterpoint to the region's lush, sea-edged woodlands.*

NORTH AMERICA

A friend from Italy once asked me to draw up a list of places she should not miss on a summer's tour of North America. Without hesitation, I wrote down the names of cities—New York and Los Angeles—and of historical sites—Boston Common and Gettysburg. My pen faltered; I put a question mark next to these initial choices and then quickly and confidently drew up the "A" list: the Grand Canyon, Baja California, the Canadian Rockies, Yellowstone National Park, the Oregon coast, the Great Smoky Mountains, the Everglades. My friend read the list, and looked up with a puzzled expression. "But hardly anyone lives in these places, do they?" she said. "And so they'll be unforgettable," I replied. "Wilderness is the soul of the continent."

What I had done was pose a North American version of the European grand tour, a journey of edification in which wilderness, still one-third of the huge continent, supplies the resonance of the past. Forests and mountains, canyons and plains: These are the palaces and cathedrals of North America. For antiquity, gaze up the column of a giant sequoia—275 feet tall and more than 25 centuries old—in the Sierra Nevada. For the sweep of time, scan the monumental walls of the Grand Canyon, where a billion years of geologic history is recorded in the colorful bands of sedimentary and metamorphic rock. For epic drama, contemplate the geysers and hot springs of Yellowstone and know that here a volcano once exploded with fiery showers of lava at the same time glaciers were advancing down nearby mountain valleys.

I cannot live happily without a journey into the North American wilderness at least once every few years. The wild places serve as sanctuaries, places in which to gulp clean air and water, to slow down time and speed up perception, to feel blessed at witnessing the finely tuned workings of nature. Whether I'm glorying in the sight of cactus blooms throwing vivid color onto a Southwest desert floor or paddling through a dark tunnel of mangroves in the Everglades, I know that my body, mind, and spirit are being recharged by the true energy sources of the continent.

Sometimes when seated in front of a campfire, unable as yet to climb into my sleeping bag because of the excitement stirred by the prospect of the next day's hike or paddle, I think about some of the early explorers in North America—Coronado, Marquette, Vancouver, Frémont. Because most of them were paving the way for civilization, they regularly described the wilderness they saw as sinister wastelands or frightening barriers. How perceptions change. Today travelers by the million make pilgrimages to the very spots these explorers visited—described now as glorious and spectacular—for the precise reason of taking a break from civilization. As campfire embers die, I usually take to bed a thought penned more than a century ago by Henry David Thoreau: "We need the tonic of wildness. . . . We can never have enough of Nature." Sleep follows like a falling star.   —*Thomas O'Neill*

Sun-warmed window of sandstone frames a skyline of mesas and buttes in Monument Valley Navajo Tribal Park, on the Arizona-Utah border. Wilderness—spectacular landforms set in lonely spaces under resplendent skies—heads the list of the continent's appealing destinations.

CANYON COUNTRY
Arizona-Utah

Artistry of erosion turns rock into bold canvases throughout the American Southwest. The hiker at left seems engulfed by a red rock sea in the Paria Canyon Wilderness Area, along the Arizona-Utah border. Surging water from desert storms etched the canyon's swirling ridges and grooves. Windblown sand helped incise the wavy patterns. Layers of more resistant stone cap the canyon walls. In Antelope Canyon (below), water has exploited a weak spot in the sandstone, cutting a narrow chasm some 150 feet deep.

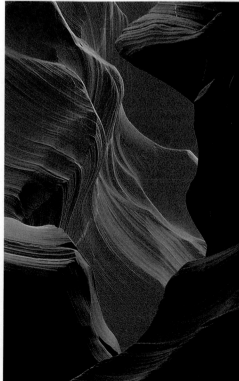

Amid steamy mangrove swamps, on waterlogged prairies, and along slow-moving channels, a wealth of sights and sounds announces the myriad creatures that inhabit southern Florida's Everglades National Park—the largest subtropical wilderness in the United States. During spring twilight, the din arising from the marshy vegetation originates from a legion of green tree frogs, their mating season having arrived. An inch-long tree frog (right) hides on an arrow arum leaf. A brown pelican (left) rests between feeding forays. As many as 300 kinds of birds frequent the Everglades, including wood storks, ibis, herons, and bald eagles. Reflected in the waters of a slough, an alligator (below) suns itself, prepared to slide off the bank in an instant. Its numbers severely reduced by hunting earlier this century, the now-protected alligator continues a strong comeback in the Florida wilds.

FRED HIRSCHMANN; KIM HEACOX (UPPER); BATES LITTLEHALES (RIGHT)

SANTA MARÍA VOLCANO
Guatemala

*S*olitary figure watches as the sun drops behind Santa María Volcano in Guatemala's Sierra Madre. One of 33 active or dormant volcanoes in the Central American country, the 12,375-foot peak erupted violently in 1902, causing ash falls as far away as 850 miles.

YUCATÁN PENINSULA
Mexico

Ruins of the Maya port city of Tulum front the Caribbean on Mexico's Yucatán Peninsula. A temple overlooks the beach where citizens greeted trading canoes laden with salt, honey, and cloth. Tulum was abandoned in the early 1500s, after the Spanish Conquest. In the Yucatán interior, a stone serpent (left) gazes toward the massive temple ruins at Chichén Itzá, once a Maya city-state.

JIM BRANDENBURG

ROCKY MOUNTAINS
Canada

D*ouble rainbow streaks the heavens in a multihued light show above the Canadian Rockies in Jasper National Park. Whether mountain world or quiet island getaway, such mirrors of earth's enchanting beauty yield the traveler's ultimate reward.* 195

Notes on Contributors

Educated in wildlife biology, TOM BEAN is a former National Park Service ranger. A free lance since 1982, he has a special interest in parklands and wilderness landscapes. He has photographed for TRAVELER magazine and the Special Publications *America's Outdoor Wonders* and *America's Hidden Wilderness.* Tom lives near Flagstaff, Arizona.

Free lance ANNIE GRIFFITHS BELT, born in Minneapolis, grew up there and earned a B.A. in photojournalism at the University of Minnesota. Since 1978 she has carried out varied assignments for the Society and has received awards for her work from the Associated Press and the National Press Photographer's Association. Annie lives near Washington, D.C.

PAUL CHESLEY resides in Aspen, Colorado, the home of the professional consortium Photographers/Aspen, which he helped establish. He has covered the Continental Divide, the West Coast forests, New Zealand, and the natural wonders of Europe for Special Publications. Paul has also contributed to TRAVELER magazine.

A founding member of Photographers/Aspen, NICHOLAS DEVORE III is the director of Galerie FotoArte and is on the board of trustees of the Aspen Art Museum. He has contributed to Society publications for 16 years. A member of the Explorers Club, he cites Bali as his most enchanting excursion and would like his next to be to Antarctica.

A science illustrator and cartographic artist, SUSAN M. JOHNSTON has a B.F.A. from Syracuse University. She was a member of the Society's staff from 1980 to 1984. Since then, she has free-lanced for Time-Life Books, Smithsonian Institution, the American Museum of Natural History, the National Arboretum, and others. Susan lives in Budd Lake, New Jersey.

A graduate of Mount Holyoke College, CHRIS ECKSTROM LEE coauthored *America's Atlantic Isles* and has written chapters for many other Special Publications, including *Mysteries of the Ancient World, Isles of the Caribbean* and *Blue Horizons: Paradise Isles of the Pacific.* She has also contributed to *Peoples and Places of the Past* and to TRAVELER magazine.

Before joining the Society's staff, PAUL MARTIN served as a military correspondent in Vietnam, edited a national boating magazine, and worked as the managing editor of a monthly medical journal. In 1979 he joined WORLD magazine as a writer-editor. For the past seven years he has been a Special Publications managing editor.

TOM MELHAM joined the Society's staff in 1971. He has written articles for NATIONAL GEOGRAPHIC magazine and has contributed to several Special Publications, including *Alaska's Magnificent Parklands, Majestic Island Worlds,* and the large-format book *The Desert Realm.* He is the author of *John Muir's Wild America.*

On the Society's staff since 1976, THOMAS O'NEILL is the author of *Back Roads America* and *Lakes, Peaks, and Prairies: Discovering the United States-Canadian Border.* Tom retraced the routes of pathfinder John Frémont for *Into the Wilderness,* journeyed to Pompeii for *Splendors of the Past,* and ventured into Australia's outback for *The Desert Realm.*

Since joining the staff in 1966, CYNTHIA RUSS RAMSAY has covered subjects related to geology, mountaineering, history, and archaeology in more than a dozen Special Publications, including *Alaska's Magnificent Parklands, Nature's World of Wonders,* and *Our Awesome Earth.* She has also served as managing editor of the Society's Books for Young Explorers.

Born in Conway, North Carolina, MEDFORD TAYLOR is a graduate of High Point College and attended graduate school at the University of Missouri. Formerly a cinematographer in Africa, he has produced photographs for WORLD, TRAVELER, and NATIONAL GEOGRAPHIC magazines. This is his first assignment for Special Publications.

JENNIFER C. URQUHART is a graduate of Smith College, where she majored in history and English. She began her career with the Society in 1971 and has since written for children's books, TRAVELER magazine, and several Special Publications, including *America's Wild and Scenic Rivers, Window On America,* and *America's Wild Woodlands.*

Library of Congress ☐P Data
Excursion to enchantment: a journey to the world's most beautiful places/prepared by the Special Publications Division, National Geographic Society, Washington, D.C.
        p.   cm.
    Bibliography: p.
    Includes index.
    ISBN 0-87044-667-3 (regular edition) ISBN 0-87044-672-X (library edition)
    1. Voyages and travels—1981-
I. National Geographic Society (U.S.).   Special Publications Division.
G465.E95 1988
910.4—dc 19   88-19520

*M*eandering brook cascades down a rocky cliffside in woods north of Franconia Notch, New Hampshire. Famous for its incandescent fall foliage, New England ranks high on the list of the world's beautiful places.

INDEX

Boldface indicates illustrations;
italic refers to picture captions.

Acknowledgments

The Special Publications Division is grateful for the assistance of the many organizations and individuals named or quoted in the text and those cited here: Marie-Odile Barthélemy, Bruce M. Bartholemew, Susan Ortiz Basualbo, Gabriel Bendersky, John Broadhead, Steve Carapetis, Robert and Marguerite Carvallo, Marie-Claude and Gérard Chauveau, Claudio Chehebar, Kathleen Crane, Thinley Dorji, Sébastien Doubinsky, Anne Durand, James Gove, Ernst Griffin, James Jahan de Lestang, Philippe Jauneaud, M. Philip Kahl, Francis Katchatouroff, Ken Leghorn, Dasho K. Letho, Paul-Jacques Lévêque-Mingam, Walter Lewis, Charlie Love, Stan MacAlister, George MacDonald, Carlos Martín, Mónica Mermoz, Bill Merrilees, Ken Mitchell, Bruce Molnia, Diana Myers, Peter Olesiuk, Barry Olsen, César Ormazábal, Richard P. Palmieri, Hans Schulz, Eduardo Scott, Isao Shiozawa, George Stuart, Ambassador Jigmi Thinley, Hubert Tissier de Mallerais, Gary Vequist, Dasho Pema Wangchuk.

Additional Reading

Readers may consult the *National Geographic Index* for related books and articles and refer to the following publications: Bruce Chatwin, *In Patagonia;* J.L. Delpal, *The Valley of the Loire Today;* Sarah Eppenbach, *Alaska's Southeast, Touring the Inside Passage;* Victor Wolfgang von Hagen, *South America Called Them;* Michelin Tourist Guide, *Châteaux of the Loire;* Alan Moorehead, *The White Nile;* Graeme Parish, *Image of Chile;* Françoise Pommaret-Imaeda and Yoshiro Imaeda, *Bhutan, A Kingdom of the Eastern Himalayas;* George Vancouver, *A Voyage of Discovery to the North Pacific Ocean and Round the World, 1791-1795;* Colin Willock, *Africa's Rift Valley.*

Composition for this book by the Typographic section of National Geographic Production Services, Pre-Press Division. Printed and bound by Holladay-Tyler Printing Corp., Rockville, Md. Film preparation by Catherine Cooke Studio, Inc., New York, N.Y. Color separations by Lanman Progressive Company, Washington, D.C.; Lincoln Graphics, Inc., Cherry Hill, N.J.; and NEC, Inc., Nashville, Tenn. Dust jacket printed by Federated Lithographers-Printers, Inc., Providence, R.I.

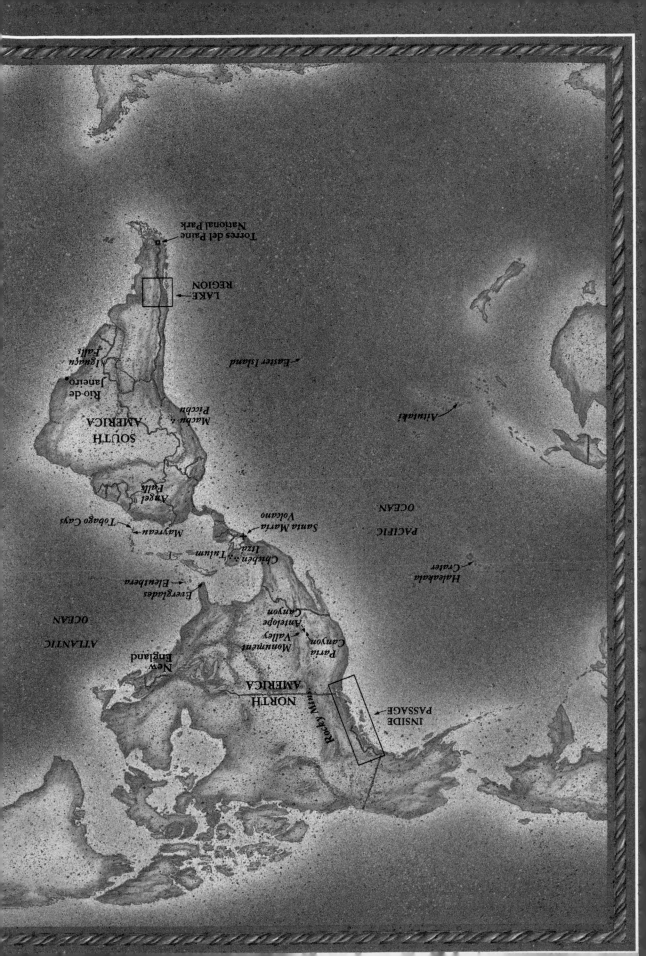